The Uses of Imperial Citizenship

Frontiers of the Political: Doing International Politics

Series Editor:

Engin Isin is Professor of International Politics, Queen Mary University of London (QMUL) and University of London Institute in Paris (ULIP). He is a leading scholar of citizenship studies and is a Chief Editor of the journal Citizenship Studies. He is author and editor of eleven books in the field, including 'Being Political' and 'Citizens Without Frontiers'.

This series aims to contribute to our understanding of transversal political struggles beyond and across the borders of the nation-state, and its institutions and mechanisms, which have become influential and effective means of both contentious politics and political subjectivity. The series features titles that eschew and even disavow interpreting these transversal political struggles with categories and concepts.

Postcolonial Transitions in Europe: Contexts, Practices, and Politics
Edited by Sandra Ponzanesi and Gianmaria Colpani

Citizenship and Place: Case Studies on the Borders of Citizenship
Edited by Cherstin M. Lyon and Allison F. Goebel

The Question of Political Community: Sameness, Logos, Space
Jonna Pettersson

Postcolonial Intellectuals in Europe: Academics, Artists, Activists, and Their Publics
Edited by Sandra Ponzanesi and Adriano José Habed

Citizen Journalism as Conceptual Practice: Postcolonial Archives and Embodied Political Acts of New Media
Bolette B. Blaagaard

Governing Affective Citizenship: Denaturalization, Belonging, and Repression
Marie Beauchamps

**Public Perception of International Crises:
Identity, Ontological Security, and Self-Affirmation**
Dmitry Chernobrov

**The Uses of Imperial Citizenship: The British and
French Empires**
Jack Harrington

The Uses of Imperial Citizenship

The British and French Empires

Jack Harrington

ROWMAN & LITTLEFIELD
Lanham • Boulder • New York • London

Published by Rowman & Littlefield
An imprint of The Rowman & Littlefield Publishing Group, Inc.
4501 Forbes Boulevard, Suite 200, Lanham, Maryland 20706
www.rowman.com

6 Tinworth Street, London SE11 5AL, United Kingdom

Copyright © 2020 by Jack Harrington

All rights reserved. No part of this book may be reproduced in any form or by any electronic or mechanical means, including information storage and retrieval systems, without written permission from the publisher, except by a reviewer who may quote passages in a review.

British Library Cataloguing in Publication Data

A catalogue record for this book is available from the British Library

ISBN 978-1-78348-920-6 (cloth: alk. paper)
ISBN 978-1-78348-922-0 (electronic)
ISBN 978-1-78348-921-3 (pbk.: alk. paper)

Library of Congress Cataloging-in-Publication Data
Names: Harrington, Jack, 1980- author.
Title: The uses of imperial citizenship : the British and French empires / Jack Harrington.
Description: Lanham, Maryland : Rowman & Littlefield Publishing Group, 2020. | Series: Frontiers of the political : doing international politics | Includes bibliographical references and index. | Summary: "Examines how ideas of citizenship and subjecthood were applied in societies under British and French imperial rule in order to expand our understanding of these concepts"—Provided by publisher.
Identifiers: LCCN 2020012608 (print) | LCCN 2020012609 (ebook) | ISBN 9781783489206 (cloth) | ISBN 9781783489220 (epub)
Subjects: LCSH: Citizenship—Great Britain—Colonies—History—19th century. | Citizenship—France—Colonies—History—19th century. | Great Britain—Colonies—Administration—History—19th century. | France—Colonies—Administration—History—19th century. | Imperialism—History—19th century. | Citizenship—Philosophy.
Classification: LCC JV1017 .H37 2020 (print) | LCC JV1017 (ebook) | DDC 324.609171/24109034—dc23
LC record available at https://lccn.loc.gov/2020012608
LC ebook record available at https://lccn.loc.gov/2020012609

Contents

Acknowledgements		ix
Introduction		1
1	Citizenship between Nation and Empire	9
2	Freedom of the Press, Liberalism and the 'Garrison-State' in British India	31
3	Citizens and Subjects in the British and French Empires	51
4	Britain and the French Invasion of Algeria, 1830–1870	69
5	Subjects across Empires	85
Conclusion		99
Notes		103
Select Bibliography		121
Index		131
About the Author		135

Acknowledgements

I would not have written this book if I had not met Engin Isin. As a research fellow at the Open University, I had the time, freedom, and encouragement to bring together my interests in the history of colonialism with contemporary sociological approaches to citizenship. Engin has been a great help with all stages of preparing this book.

Most of the research for this book was undertaken while I was at the Open University, as part of 'Oecumene: Citizenship after Orientalism' funded by the European Research Council (grant number 249379). I am much obliged to the Oecumene team for a fantastic and fun research environment. Thank you to Alessandra Marino, Amandine Scherrer, Andrea Mura, Anne Paynter, Aya Ikagame, Dana Rubin, Deena Dajani, Iker Barbero, Leticia Sabsay, Lisa Pilgram, Radha Ray, Tara Atluri, and Zaki Nahaboo. I would also like to thank all of my colleagues on the *Citizenship Studies* editorial team for encouraging me on my continuing journey in the world of studying citizenship. Catherine Hall, Alan Lester, David Johnson, Gavin Murray-Miller, and Raia Prokhovnik kindly read or commented on earlier drafts of some of the chapters in this book. Judith Becker enabled me to present a very early version of my idea for this book to the Leibniz Institute of European History in January 2014. I would like to thank Olena Heywood for her careful and insightful reading of the whole manuscript.

I wish to thank the team at Rowman & Littlefield International, particularly Dhara Snowden and Rebecca Anastasi; I am grateful for your interest in the book and for your patience with the final stages. I have had quite a few other obligations while writing this book and would like to thank David Coombe and Jon Deer at the London School of Economics and Dan O'Connor at the Wellcome Trust for the interest and support they have provided. Finally, many, many thanks to Sophie Heywood and Lena Heywood Harrington.

Introduction

In the years following World War II, the philosopher Hannah Arendt wrote *Origins of Totalitarianism* (1951). In this work, she attempted to understand why Europe had experienced the horrors of totalitarianism. Part of the answer lay in the history of what she called 'imperialism', which fostered the forms of violence and racism that would be associated with totalitarianism. In her view, imperialism—as opposed to empire-building—had turned ideas associated with business such as expansion and competition into axioms of political action.[1] In 1917, Vladimir Lenin had called imperialism the highest stage of capitalism. Wryly, Arendt labeled it 'the first stage of the political rule of the bourgeoisie'.[2] For Arendt, the high imperialism of the late nineteenth century ruptured a division between the history of the nation-state and that of European imperial conquest. This parallel history, she argued, had been in evidence since the French Revolution, during which colonial conquest had been rejected as a source of corruption. As Arendt saw it, the empire-building that Britain pursued for much of the nineteenth century followed the Greek model of colonization, involving settlers and limited efforts to integrate native populations. The French in contrast pursued Roman imperialism, incorporating Algeria, for example, as a Department of France.[3]

Arendt's account is both schematic and very much of its time. Her damning critique of European imperialism as the precursor of the excesses of twentieth-century Europe draws on a number of assumptions. First, the idea of an essentially separate history of both the nation-state and European colonialism draws on a long established and still influential historiography which argues that Britain in particular acquired its empire 'in a fit of absent-mindedness'.[4] In other words, these were separate developments with colonialism barely capable of having any impact on the nation-state for much of its history. Secondly, it offers a clear-cut and rather caricatured contrast between a liberal and colonial Britain and a republican and imperial France. Even excoriating critiques of European imperialism and its impact, such as Arendt provided, carry within them a set of assumptions that are themselves a product of empire.

Modern citizenship in the west has been shaped by the history of empire as much as that of the nation-state. So much of what citizenship involves in national contexts such as those of Britain and France can only be understood through histories that fully integrate colonial experience. Many features of citizenship as an institution owe their formation to colonial government. These include the designation of certain groups within a state as minorities; the assertion of citizenship rights by new migrant populations; the recurrent withdrawal of fundamental rights from particular groups; the conferral of supranational citizenship rights; and the history of 'western liberalism' in postcolonial nations. These complex phenomena are central to contemporary citizenship. Yet normative models of citizenship still rely largely on national histories and on a repertoire of rights, obligations, and actions derived from a narrowly rendered Euro-American historical experience. This is true of much scholarship about the history of such 'western' institutions in postcolonial societies. To describe citizenship, for example, as a kind of import or imposition is to underplay the extent to which aspects of citizenship owe their origins to colonial rule. European colonial domination was an integral aspect of the formation of citizenship as understood in the west.

The example of Britain and France is instructive. Both are cited as the models for liberal and republican traditions of citizenship, respectively. They were also the two largest western European colonial powers of the nineteenth and twentieth centuries. It is clear that the two phenomena are not only related but also contingent. The decades between the 1830s and 1950s witnessed both the transformation of the imperial projects of these powers and the constitution of what we would recognize as a modern citizenship regime. The differences between ideas of the citizen, state, and society in Britain and France have been seen to reflect a division between liberal and republican traditions of citizenship.

The ways in which these traditions were shaped by the experience of colonialism in the nineteenth and twentieth centuries have seldom been studied singly, let alone comparatively or as a series of connections or commonalities.

The Uses of Imperial Citizenship examines the ways in which ideas of citizenship and subjecthood were shaped by the domination of large colonial populations. It does so by taking examples from the experience of the British and French empires. More radically, it examines the ways in which claims to the rights and obligations of imperial subjects by people otherwise pushed to the margins, from women activists to 'native' newspaper editors, shaped the history of British and French citizenship regimes.[5] Analytically, it is clear that the borders of empires do not mark the boundaries of those forms of knowledge creation that generated practices and discourses associated with imperial domination. Examples include orientalism, biological racism, or the reconstitution of international legal norms to rule over non-European peoples.[6] *The Uses of Imperial Citizenship* examines such connections through the example of British and French imperial enterprises to show that 'European-ness' was itself fractured along national cultural lines and constituted through such ventures. In doing this, it will show how citizenship as a national or European institution can only fully be understood in the context of empire.

The focus of *The Uses of Imperial Citizenship* is the governing of colonial societies within, on the frontiers of, and outside of citizenship and subjecthood as institutions. More than a conventional comparative history of similarities and differences, the book points to associations and contrasts expressed by contemporaries themselves. Its aim is not to provide a comprehensive history or comparison of the British and French experience, but rather to use both together to elucidate the complexities of imperial citizenship. This is done through extensive analysis of colonial and diplomatic archives, parliamentary debates and commissions, journalism, and contemporary works conducted on colonial administration. *The Uses of Imperial Citizenship* also draws together a significant body of academic literature in French and English on different aspects of colonial experience, including the extensive and sophisticated francophone debate on the nature of citizenship (only a limited sample of which is available in translation). To provide conceptual and empirical coherence, the book concentrates for the most part on examples from French Algeria and British India. This enables more comparisons across sites where imperial citizenship was constituted and greater depth of analysis than would be possible in a book that aims solely at geographical comprehensiveness.

The Uses of Imperial Citizenship is divided into five chapters. The first chapter sketches out the conceptual implications of understanding the history of colonialism in terms of citizenship. When understood as a set of rights and obligations, citizenship has been seen both as a western historical formation forcibly inherited by postcolonial nations and as something more general, the history of which can be written on a global scale. This chapter argues that European colonialism was an essential element of the formation of citizenship as understood in the West. By seeing it as something already formed and then imposed on another society, we underestimate the extent to which aspects of citizenship owe their origins to colonial rule. This claim creates a challenge of how to write a history of the colonial contexts of citizenship that can account for the exclusion and acts of resistance that were such significant aspects of it. This chapter does so by taking ways of analyzing the dynamics of contemporary citizenship and applying them to the history of colonialism. An account of the formation of contemporary citizenship rooted in colonial history supports the argument that citizenship is defined by what it excludes as much as by what it includes. Moreover, the idea of the citizen is changeable and contested. Through this approach, the book aims to inform the study of contemporary struggles over citizenship.

The second chapter offers a detailed example of the role the imperial rule had in shaping aspects of what it considered to be European or western liberal ideas. It takes what is seen to be a key historic right of the contemporary democratic citizen and explores how it unfolded in a context of imperial rule in British India. The history of freedom of the press in British India is one that was not contingent on representative government. Debates over restrictions on press freedom in India between 1799 and their repeal in 1835 should be seen as part of the growth of liberal rights regimes in the nineteenth century. The operation of English law (rather than Hindu or Muslim codes), on 'non-Europeans' in this context, revealed the inherent conflict between executive power and the rule of law. This tension was a key feature of British colonial rule in India as a rights regime. The freedom of the press, understood as integral to the protection of liberty and scrutiny of executive power, become a crucible for this contest. The struggle between the authorities,

Indian and European newspaper editors, and the law courts revealed tensions between the supposed rights of the British subject and the freedoms permitted under imperial rule. It did so in ways that subverted, as much as they reaffirmed, the formal divisions made between Indians and Europeans. In this sense, the claiming of press freedom in the context of empire and the absence of representative government invites us to provincialize the metropolitan context of British liberal thought. The chapter is a contribution to a history of rights in the context of empire.

The third chapter significantly broadens the scope of analysis to sketch a history of the formation of imperial citizenship across the British and French empires. It challenges conventional accounts of the distinctions between both French and British concepts of the citizen and between the metropolitan and colonial courses of those histories. It establishes that examples from both the British and French empires can be used to identify certain common features of imperial citizenship (as distinct from national citizenship). Rather than offering a set of comparisons and contrasts between types of citizenship or practices of empire, this approach views the British and French empires as part of a common history. In the first half of the nineteenth century—the subject of this book—Britain and France were, for much of the time, key exponents of European liberalism. Historical narratives that have emphasized the contrasts between British and French approaches to empire downplay a lack of uniformity in each case and the common features of their colonial rule. A sketch of this joint history is provided in the chapter to explore how these variations across empires reveal more commonalities than differences in the constitution of imperial citizens.

The fourth chapter offers a detailed example of this joint history by examining British perceptions of the French invasion and conquest of Algeria. Numerous British commentators—including travellers, diplomats, and mercenaries—drew comparisons between the French in Algeria and the British Empire. The conquest raised issues to do with military government and the management of local populations that invited references to British India. At the same time, French efforts to promote settler colonialism encouraged reflections on settler societies in Canada, Australia, and New Zealand. The British response to the French invasion of Algeria prompted reflections on the nature of imperial rule and the management of colonial populations. As imperial powers, Britain and France were seen by these commentators as engaged in a common enterprise, in similar circumstances. This made comparisons of forms of imperial subjugation and population management possible and desirable. Such writings describe contrasts and differences, but they also articulate a sense of a civilizational imperative shared by France and Britain as the vanguard of advanced commercial society and as colonial powers. This adds to the coherence of imperial subjecthood and imperial rule as forms and practices that transcended national difference as part of a common European enterprise.

The fifth chapter examines one of the most important ways in which the limits of imperial citizenship were revealed. Claiming rights as someone moving across borders is a fundamental aspect of modern citizenship particularly as supranational versions such as EU Citizenship continue to develop in complexity and importance. The protection granted to individuals by their government when they were abroad was one of the defining features of belonging to the British or French Empire. It continues to be a hallmark of contemporary citizenship. This chapter examines how imperial citizenship was constituted through movement not only within but also between empires. The confluence of empires in the Mediterranean in the early nineteenth century provides rich examples of the ways in which such protection was negotiated. Shifting Ottoman, French, and British authorities, combined with migration flows of different populations, gave rise to forms of imperial control and subjecthood characterized by movement across borders. These included the granting of protection by imperial powers and the application of norms governing conduct between different empires. In this case, the invasion of Algiers transformed those lands into the colonial possessions of a western European or, to use contemporary language, 'Christian' power. The chapter uses consular records for Algiers to see how the rights and protections of British subjects outside of British territory were enacted, particularly in the context of the transfer of the territory to a fellow Christian power. Crucially, as the example shows, the right to protection was not simply a fixed body of rules to be applied. It raised ambiguities that required judgment about appropriate norms. It was such negotiations in themselves that constituted the right to protection. This inconsistent, fluid formation of the norms and practices of subjecthood as a way of regulating mobility is a key aspect of what later became modern citizenship.

The concluding chapter draws together observations from the book as a whole to examine the strains placed on imperial citizenship as a medium of belonging and for the claiming of rights. It examines how alternative ways of being political or of claiming social and civil rights came about in opposition to a reforming and more inclusive model of imperial citizenship. *The Uses of Imperial Citizenship* concludes by analyzing the connection between the terminal decline of imperial citizenship and the ascent of a social model of national citizenship in Britain and France.

The Uses of Imperial Citizenship opens up new ways to understand the historical formation of contemporary citizenship. Examples have been drawn from a significant period in the history of citizenship and the history of empire of two European nations. These can only be applied more generally to a very limited degree. However, they reveal aspects of colonial experience that form what would become known as citizenship. Citizenship should be seen as an institution or set of practices that is derived, at least in large part, from the empire-state as much as the nation-state. This lens is particularly useful if we seek to understand key aspects of citizenship today, particularly as an instrument of group differentiation and exclusion. At the same time, if we understand citizenship in the present as something dynamic—something that can be conferred, taken away, and redefined—this necessitates a continual reexamining of its origins.

Chapter 1

Citizenship between Nation and Empire

I

Throughout the nineteenth and twentieth centuries, millions of people lived under the British and French empires in every inhabited continent. Formal status varied considerably, so too did the ways in which those people acted politically and attempted to claim civil and social rights. For some, because empire was chiefly characterized by domination, it deprived colonial populations of any substantive field for political belonging except through resistance and rebellion.[1] In fact, these aspects of colonial rule can tell us a great deal about the ways in which contemporary citizenship regimes entrenched inequality. In the extensive and diffuse scholarly literature on the European empires, stark lines have been drawn to distinguish between the more and less privileged under empire: these include white and non-white, European and non-European, citizen and subject, and, perhaps most famously, the colonizer and the colonized. Most can be traced to historic uses of such terms. To some extent, these may appear to be different ways of observing similar distinctions. Yet when we recount the history of citizenship through empire, the fluid and contested nature of political belonging becomes evident. The formal assertion of control and the operating of forms and instruments of government that went with it, such as citizenship status, give only a partial explanation of how societies have functioned in the context of imperial rule.

A fairly well-known example may illustrate the point. A boy born in 1930 in Algiers to Jewish parents of Spanish origin was, at the point of his birth, a French citizen. At the age of eleven, he was deprived of his citizenship, becoming instead a French subject. In 1943, his status was restored. From the age of thirty-two, he would have only been able to claim citizenship of the land in which he was born if he gave up his French citizenship to become a citizen of Algeria. This is the story of Jacques Derrida, one of the most famous French philosophers of the twentieth century. At birth he had been a French citizen, because, in 1870, the Crémieux Decree had granted French Citizenship to all Jews from Algeria.[2] In 1940, the Vichy regime repealed the Crémieux Decree, depriving Jews in Algeria of their French citizenship. It was restored following the taking of Algeria by the Free French forces, although not immediately.[3] When Algeria declared independence in 1962, Derrida would only have been able to have Algerian Citizenship if he had renounced his French Citizenship. In *The Monolingualism of the Other*, Derrida himself noted:

> The concept of group or class can no longer give rise to a simple topic of exclusion, inclusion, or belonging. This quasi–subgroup will then be that of 'indigenous Jews,' as they were then called. Being French citizens from 1870 until the laws of exclusion of 1940, they could not properly identify themselves, in the double sense of 'identifying oneself' and 'identifying one–self with' the other.

Derrida's case illustrates the defining features of the operation of the status of citizenship. It raises common themes in the history of citizenship generally and of its colonial contexts in particular. Significant in this case was that his parents were identified as Jews. The granting of citizenship to Jews *en masse* implied that there was sufficient compatibility between their social values and practices and those expected of French citizens for them to be considered suitable for French citizenship. The Crémieux Decree, issued in the first months of Third Republic, aimed to strengthen the fledgling regime at a stroke by creating French citizenships out of the Algerian Jewish population. Under the Vichy regime, this was reversed. As Gérard Noiriel, a pioneering historian of migration in France, has observed, the inclusion of Jews into French society has depended on the extent to which they have been viewed as foreigners.[4] Pap Ndiaye has made similar observations about the experience of being black in contemporary France.[5] These examples speak to what Derrida described as 'the artifice and precariousness of citizenship'.[6] The identifying of groups outside the dominant group as compatible or incompatible with political belonging is a common aspect of debate throughout the histories of the British and French empires. Equally, as this example shows, independence from imperial rule is not simply the separation of a national identity from that of an empire—it is the rupturing of colonial identity.

Even decades after the formal end of empire, the ambiguities and precarity of postcolonial citizenship remain part of life in former colonial states such as Britain and France. In April 2018, the *Guardian* newspaper reported on the treatment of many in the 'Windrush generation' of postwar migrants from former colonies to the United Kingdom. It described the plight of 'retirement-age citizens who have lived and paid taxes in the UK for decades, have been detained, made homeless, sacked or denied benefits and NHS [National Health Service] treatment because they have struggled to prove they are British'.[7] As this harrowing recent example demonstrates, there is a dissonance between layers of formal citizenship and how citizenship is lived, experienced, and practiced. This is an aspect of citizenship under the nation-state, but it also points to the imperfection and impermanence of breaks with the colonial past.[8]

How the history of citizenship is traced and what stories are told about its origins have also varied considerably from polity to polity and across time. Citizenship is a constantly reinvented tradition because there are struggles over its scope and effects. Familiar narratives of European citizenship that retread an old path from ancient Greece, via Italian city-states and the American and French revolutions, are the result of contracted ideological conflict over what contemporary citizenship meant at any one time.[9] This inherited narrative of the history of citizenship in the west belies its own fractious formation. It is a vision of the past that acknowledges the different sources that constitute European citizenship. At the same time, with the notable exception of the American Revolution, it renders colonial experience a supplement to that history. It has little to tell us about the ways in which polities beyond the borders of Europe, such as settler states, colonial possessions, and independent powers all contributed to the formation of contemporary citizenship. It is worth asking why a certain set of rights-claiming activities in a certain sequence of geographic and historic contents come to be understood as the history of citizenship in the west.

There is a tension between the narrow framing of citizenship as membership of a nation-state and the sheer range of types of polities and contexts to which citizens today belong. Narratives of the western experience that restrict themselves to events in Europe fail to account for the emergence of elements that are integral to the experience of citizens across much of the world today. These include the labeling of certain groups within a state as minorities; the assertion of citizenship rights by new migrant populations; and the recurrent withdrawal of fundamental rights from particular groups (e.g., Jews throughout European history) and the conferral of supranational citizenship rights (such as European Union citizenship). These complex phenomena are central to contemporary citizenship. Yet normative models of citizenship still rely largely on national histories and on a repertoire of rights, obligations, and actions seen to derive from a narrowly rendered Euro-American historical experience.[10] Domination, deprivation of rights, and other aspects of colonial politics are part of the history of contemporary citizenship as experienced in former colonial and colonized polities. The problems that beset and characterize what is seen as the western tradition of citizenship, such as exclusion, inequality, and identity-based prejudice, are best understood through a common history of citizenship across the boundaries of contemporary nation-states.

Recognition of these aspects of the historical formation of citizenship requires a dynamic understanding of what citizenship is, how it is constituted, and how it changes over time. This has been a central concern of critical citizenship studies. The principal writers in this vein and their ideas will be discussed in more detail later. According to this approach, the question of what comprises citizenship cannot be adequately captured by definitions that see citizenship simply as a status or as a set of rights and obligations that are conferred, imposed, or withheld. Who can be a citizen and what actions are considered appropriate to that status change over time and in different contexts. There is a necessary corollary between a definition of who can be counted as a citizen and what would be considered behavior befitting a citizen. In other words, who is a citizen and what kinds of actions define one are linked. Moreover, the idea of the citizen is constituted together with the idea of the non-citizen. This creates a context or site for contest over who can be called a citizen. Contestation is a constant characteristic of citizenship, as the right to be considered a citizen is successfully claimed. Scholars working within critical citizenship studies would argue that such change is driven by practice or action. Building on this understanding of contemporary citizenship, I do not find an explanation of the nature of citizenship in the mapping of changes in status and of what that status entails in terms of rights and obligations. Instead, my approach here is to understand it as an institution constituted through practice and actions.

A key feature of this chapter and of this book is to apply an approach informed by critical citizenship studies to the historical formation of citizenship during the zenith of two major European imperial powers: Britain and France. Significantly, for much of the nineteenth century, Britain and France were also seen to be crucibles of the political and civil reform that are now understood to characterize modern western citizenship. My aim in undertaking this analysis is to provide an approach to understanding the history of colonialism that enlists many of the most useful analytical tools of contemporary citizenship studies. These include recognizing that categories of group identification are fluid and under constant reconstitution; identifying political action as broadly as possible, beyond the limited repertoires of formal representation; and providing a sophisticated rendering of how subjugated or marginalized peoples are constituted as outsiders within a society. At the same time, I hope to provide an historical explanation that gives a better account of these features of contemporary citizenship than the received narrative of citizenship in the West.

Later chapters in this book will explore particular features of imperial citizenship. The first chapter sets out to elaborate how and why citizenship has been understood as a category in the history of western political thought and experience. Further explanation will be given as to what is meant here by 'citizenship'. The central argument is that the examples of colonial France and Britain suggest the political forms of modernity were not formed in the nation-states of northern Europe and then exported to their colonial possessions. The following section challenges not only conventional Euro-centric histories but also aspects of its postcolonial critique. As will be argued, this is not so much a history of the context of the specific uses and meaning of the word 'citizen', rather it is a history of those aspects of belonging to a polity that are now seen to constitute citizenship. The development of citizenship as a category and of what constitutes being or not being a citizen was a product of colonialism as much as of modern nation-state formation. The next section will review the analytical tools that have been developed to understand contemporary citizenship and sketch how these can be applied to a synoptic study of political belonging and colonialism in the British and French empires. In this way, citizenship is used as an example of more general patterns in the history of modern political concepts and their colonial legacies.

II

Drawing together the history of European empires with that of western nations uproots entrenched ways of thinking about citizenship. Perhaps the most obvious of these established ideas concerns conceiving citizenship as a product of western historical experience subsequently exported to the rest of the world, often with force and with damaging structural legacies such as statelessness.[11] Regardless of the extent to which one agrees with this view of the origins of contemporary citizenship, the presumption of its validity has profoundly shaped both the experience and the historical assessment of citizenship in the context of European imperialism and its aftermath. It has been a prominent aspect of academic and political debates about legacies of colonialism.

In Britain and France, historical writing about empire and contemporary politics have been intertwined at regular intervals. In the first decades of the twenty-first century, the historiography of both British and French imperial history has been absorbed by the relationship between the colonial past and domestic and global politics in the present. For British and American historiography in particular, the 2003 U.S. invasion of Iraq encouraged stark reflections on how the history of empire offers lessons for the present. These ranged from the celebratory to the censorious in works written for both general and specialist audiences. In the succeeding decade, the Conservative Secretary of State Education in the United Kingdom, Michael Gove, attempted to introduce a school curriculum that did more to actively celebrate the British past, including aspects of imperial history.[12] In France during the same period, scholarly writing on the colonial past was linked even more directly to political debates in the present. In 2005, the French National Assembly passed a law, Article 4 of which called upon teachers in French *lycées* to 'recognise and acknowledge the positive role of the French presence abroad particularly in North Africa'.[13] The law provoked public condemnation from intellectuals and historians, including Aimé Césaire, Marc Ferro, and Benjamin Stora, and was partially repealed the following year. This intersection of colonial history and contemporary politics was by no means new in France. Writing in 1998, Adrian Favell observed, 'The decolonization struggles and the shift towards more critical approaches in the social sciences and philosophy hardly seem to have shaken the republican commitment to the French *mission civilisatrice*. The latter has been, in a sense, reinvented within the bounds of the post-colonial European nation-state'.[14] The opening years of the twenty-first century have witnessed a self-consciously politicized academic investigation of the colonial past.

Former colonial nations have also grappled with the political legacy of colonialism in a way that shapes the politics of contemporary scholarship. There has been a tension between nation-building in the present and the complex legacy of colonial and precolonial practices, laws, and norms. The quest for a form of citizenship or other kind of political belonging that rejects fealty to an imperial polity and invigorates a postcolonial nation has been a feature of much postcolonial theory. This can be seen in the reading of its own antecedents, in the nationalist writings of authors such as Jomo Kenyatta, Ho Chi Minh, and Jawaharlal Nehru. Frantz Fanon, writing on the eve of Algerian Independence, saw nationalism as the inevitable expression of anticolonialism, regretting that other forms of solidarity between colonized peoples could not immediately take its place.[15] Much writing that identifies itself in this vein stresses that the task of building the postcolonial nation has been both necessitated and frustrated by the political structures of the colonial state. If empire is marked by the absence of political autonomy and by subjugation generally, then the postcolonial nation can easily be presented as the antidote to this, to the extent that it promises a substantive citizenship. The rights and obligations of the citizen can only be fully realized with the emergence of the postcolonial nation-state.

An earlier historiography associated with the first generation of postcolonial theorists in the latter part of the twentieth century labeled citizenship, along with other 'modern concepts', as western impositions on colonized peoples. Writing in 1993, Gayatri Chakravorty Spivak called citizenship one of several urgent political claims in decolonized space 'coded within the legacy of imperialism'. In an often-cited passage, she noted, 'What is being effectively reclaimed is a series of regulative political concepts whose supposedly authoritative narrative of production was written elsewhere, in the social formations of Western Europe. They are thus being reclaimed, indeed claimed, as concept-metaphors for which no historically adequate referent may be advanced from postcolonial space'.[16] Spivak presents citizenship as something inadequate for, or inappropriate to, postcolonial society because it has been severed from its original historical context in the west.

This prompts a question about how the historical formation of citizenship interweaves with the experience of colonialism. Does citizenship refer to an essentially western tradition or to something more universal or adaptable that can somehow be salvaged from any particular social formation, such as that of Europe? A common criticism of the latter approach is of course that the supposedly universalist language of citizenship is in fact a feature of its Eurocentrism.[17] Attempts have been made to write a common history of the diverse and ontologically distinct traditions and cultures that have fed into various manifestations of what would otherwise be called western political concepts.[18] However, my concern is with the revision of histories of western citizenship. The idea of 'citizenship' as a European export provides only a very limited explanation of its history in the context of empire and decolonization. Many of the features of contemporary citizenship in postcolonial societies, and also in those of former colonial powers, can be traced to the colonial past. My aim is to provide specific historic examples from the British and French empires that indicate how contemporary western citizenship has been shaped by the experience of colonialism.

To treat citizenship as something formed in Europe and then imposed elsewhere presents it as a closed historical development. This has a number of implications that limit our ability to grasp the nuances of the legacy of colonialism. First, it suggests that the geographical focus of its development is narrowly contained, say for example 'in the social formations of Western Europe'. Under this schema, certain geographical shifts in focus occur. For example, the point of interest moves from the city-states of Italy of the sixteenth century, on to Britain and its North American colonies and then to revolutionary France in the seventeenth and eighteenth centuries. The coterminous origins of European citizenship and European colonial expansion are often seen as mutually constitutive but still geographically distinct. This is a feature, for instance, in narratives of dependency and capital drain which assume that the stability, prosperity, and thus the political culture of 'the west' was built on an aggressively extractive capitalist imperialism that entrenched poverty across what is now called the Global South.[19] An extensive scholarship connects the growth of civil and political rights in Europe and its settler colonies with an experimental, improving attitude to government and commerce that characterized the liberal nineteenth century.[20] The growth in global or transnational histories has only partially disrupted this vision of key concepts such as citizenship.[21]

Secondly, citizenship has been presented as closed in the sense that it is a largely finished project or at least so advanced that most major groups have been or are in the process of integration into the model of citizenship.[22] The assumption here is that citizenship's formation in national contexts is essentially a filling out of the universalist claims of its status, moving beyond exclusions based on property ownership, gender, and race.[23] As Étienne Balibar and Paul Gilroy among others have noted, this account of the history of citizenship limits the sense of political legitimacy within the national project of immigrant or postcolonial populations in states such as France and Britain.[24] Analytically, the idea of citizenship and integration as closed or near finished projects has been an important way of accounting for the failure of western nation-states to adequately accommodate the legitimate rights-claims of contemporary marginalized groups. This rendering of the history of citizenship has been a common feature of both narrow western historical scholarship and of its postcolonial critique.

Colonial settings can be understood as locales where many 'western concepts' were effectively constituted.[25] The empire-states of the nineteenth and twentieth century raised questions of who could and could not be a citizen that cannot adequately be explained by a narrative of their social formation located solely in Euro-America. As Frederick Cooper has observed, politics under empire cannot meaningfully be reduced to a colonial and the anticolonial.[26] If we respond in earnestness to the challenge laid down by Balibar and Gilroy, the formalization of difference conferred by the status of citizenship can demonstrate how colonialism has shaped it as an institution, which is an aspect of French republican citizenship that will be discussed in the next chapter. My point here is not to refute portrayals of empire as a form of domination or exploitation, or even of imposition. Rather, these are prominent parts of a common legacy of citizenship, one that the ontological assumption of difference between colonized and colonizer elides.

An investigation of the connection between the historical formation of western citizenship and colonialism must therefore move beyond such a thin model of difference. A useful model can be found in Anthony Anghie's work on how 'western international law' is not most usefully understood as a regime imposed on the world through

European expansion, but as the operation of colonialism. As he observes, 'Colonialism was not an example of the application of sovereignty; rather, sovereignty was constituted through colonialism'.[27] Jon Wilson has made a similar point about the growth of imperial government in South Asia from the late eighteenth century onward. Wilson adapts Talal Asad's understanding of 'modernity', describing it as 'a state of affairs which people try to bring into existence in the future'. '"The project" of modern statehood', he observes, 'emerged from political and semantic crises occurring in colonial South Asia: it was not an export of European society'.[28] Wilson and Anghie show the value of rejecting the idea of a coherent set of ideas travelling from their point of origin to a new and unsuitable context. Analytically, this moves us beyond explanations rooted in the imposition of 'Western' ontologies on a passive or under-described colonized 'East'.[29] The logic of this move is not to downplay oppression, domination, and the entrenchment of inequality as aspects of imperialism but to better explain them and their legacy.

An historical investigation into citizenship's imperial antecedents risks emphasizing a certain kind of cosmopolitan experience. It can easily become a history of how some colonial elites and professional groups adopted and affected political language and legal forms associated with colonial powers. This is a criticism that has been leveled at attempts to write global history such as C. A. Bayly's *Birth of the Modern World* published in 2004.[30] As Jeremy Adelman puts it, 'It is hard not to conclude that global history is another Anglospheric invention to integrate the Other into a cosmopolitan narrative on our terms, in our tongues'.[31] Significant contributions to this topic such as Sukanya Banerjee's *Becoming Imperial Citizens* and Daniel Gorman's *Imperial Citizenship* or even Fredrick Cooper's study of the postwar French colonies, *Between Empire and Nation*, occupy themselves primarily with how certain elite and exceptional individuals conceptualized their place in an imperial order. My own work does not entirely escape this criticism. I believe such approaches have value if integrated with narratives that fully account for both everyday practices and the politics of protest and resistance. This requires tools from other fields such as critical citizenship studies. Moreover, these narratives of the citizen under empire can all help to inform a vision of contemporary citizenship that acknowledges the extent to which colonialism and empire are imbricated in its origin.

The formal exclusion of certain populations from the rights of a particular status, such as 'citizen', does not render them marginal to the story of how that citizenship was formed. As Eduardo Mendieta has said, 'Citizenship is a legal canopy built over centuries of struggles'.[32] Such struggles are a consequence of the fact that the citizen is, in Spivak's words, 'a regulative concept'. They have been an aspect of the development of the nation-state. One can see this in trends such as the enfranchisement of certain groups. One can point to the 'Jewish Emancipation' in nineteenth-century France and Britain or the gaining of the vote by women in the twentieth century after decades of rights claiming. When applied to the history of the British and French empires, how can this approach incorporate a robust understanding of aspects of imperial rule such as the severe restriction of formal rights, the displacement and destruction of populations, and organized resistance against colonial rule? Colonial struggles are a necessary part of this historical rendering of citizenship. Political groupings such as the Aligarh movement in late nineteenth-century India or the interwar Young Algerians have been viewed as proto-nationalist or as failed alternatives to anticolonial nationalism.[33] However, their efforts to claim rights under colonial rule should be read as aspects of the operation of imperial citizenship. The same is true of early nineteenth-century examples discussed later in this book, such as the 'native' editors of newspapers in British India and the Maltese and North African Jewish claimants of British protection in French Algiers. Moreover, as all these examples show, such rights claiming often pushed existing boundaries of imperial belonging, reconstituting it.

Even if we limit ourselves to the histories of Britain and France and their former settler colonies, it is clear that colonized peoples have been a significant aspect of that history. To the extent that citizenship in colonies differed from the experience of it in metropolitan contexts, key factors include the greater possibility of experimentation; the apparent necessity for new technologies of government because of distance or limited resources; new scales of population differentiation and management; and the prevalence and scale of violent and other forms of coercion. The dyad between exclusion and inclusion, between colonizer and colonized lacks explanatory power without a dynamic sense of how these struggles over citizenship have played out.

III

A significant body of critical literature about contemporary citizenship advances the idea that citizenship is never merely conferred, it is claimed. If among those to whom citizenship is granted we can identify the active and the passive, we can also go further and talk of those to whom it is not conferred, who claim it through their actions.[34] This line of thinking can be traced, among other sources, to Hannah Arendt's discussion of 'the right to have rights' as a critical site for political contest. The use of mechanisms for claiming rights—such as lobbying, legal action, protest, or resistance—has led historically to the expansion of who can be called a citizen. More importantly for our present purposes, struggles for inclusion or recognition only provide a partial explanation of the historic dynamic of citizenship. As Engin Isin has noted in *Being Political*, 'The logic of exclusion based on establishing opposite others is only one among countless strategies open to the formation of identities'. With reference to the philosopher Emmanuel Levinas, Isin explains, 'That is why it is important to distinguish between the logics of alterity that constitute strangers and outsiders as immanent identities and the logics of exclusion and enclosure that constitute aliens or barbarians as transitive or exterior identities'.[35] For Isin, this aspect of citizenship's history has been elided in nineteenth- and twentieth-century accounts of its history. His point here is that such accounts have noted the addition of groups to the ranks of the citizenry without fully acknowledging the ways in which their previous exclusion had been a defining aspect of citizenship. Isin goes further, suggesting that the constitution of certain groups of excluded peoples has been a function of citizenship.

If this is relevant to the history of the nation-state, it seems essential to our understanding of how national and colonial contexts are viewed together. A principal aim of this book is to present a number of historical accounts that acknowledge the role of the immanent identities of non-citizens in the constitution of the citizen. Looking at the history of citizenship under imperial rule, one might reasonably ask, why study a form of political belonging from which most people in a society would be excluded or under which nominal membership of a polity is accompanied by severe restrictions on rights. As contemporary critical citizenship studies suggest, a major point of interest in studying 'imperial citizenship' is the constitution of those who are in some respects excluded but are still in other senses part of the group—for example, nationals or colonial subjects but not citizens. In talking about contemporary society, Isin identifies those who are 'constituted as permanent outsiders, who are unreformable and unalterable, and thus either unwilling or incapable of conducting themselves as citizens. This, in turn, justifies . . . alienating technologies such as intimidation, deportation, banning, surveillance, and immobilization'. Here, Isin is referring to contemporary political discourse about law and order but the pattern he articulates is useful for thinking about historic societies as well.

At a glance, this analytical lens may appear to reveal little that is not already made plain in postcolonial and decolonial scholarship. All are involved in a kind of 're-centering'. They bring to the fore political actions and political subjects that have been on the margins. Recalling Spivak, a limitation one could observe regarding critical citizenship studies would be its insistence on the centrality of citizenship, a narrowly framed regulative political concept. In retaining the figure of the citizen, arguably critical citizenship limits itself to the study of a restrictive and exclusionary institution, because it emphasizes membership. One could make the same point about the use of 'citizenship' in historical studies of political belonging and the claiming of rights. Crucially, a key feature of critical citizenship studies is its preoccupation with the mutability both of the institution of citizenship and of what counts as political action. As Nyers and Isin have noted, using Derrida's deployment of the idea of being 'under erasure', 'It demands a disposition that is both, and yet not quite, after the past and before the future. Far from being politically debilitating, the indeterminacy of this orientation allows for the negotiation of many of citizenship's paradoxes and ambivalences'.[36] The full implications of this are worth spelling out. Isin's rejection of the primacy of inclusion and exclusion depends on a dynamic model of citizenship. As Clarke, Coll, Dagnino, and Neveu note, if 'inclusion' is not rejected, then a broader conception of it must be used. ' "Inclusion" can be conceived in two different ways: as a process through which the very definition of this polity and its constitutive dimensions is collectively redefined; or as inclusion in an already defined polity, the fundamental elements of which are not to be challenged'. As they observe, the latter has been the dominant view, and I would argue a reason for the rejection of citizenship. But if we are to understand the persistence of citizenship as a way in which politics is enacted, then we require a method that keeps the formation of citizenship as its main concern while recognizing that one of its key features as an historic phenomenon is the reconstitution of what it means. Who can be a citizen, what do citizens do, and what polity must they be citizens of have all been matters of significant negotiation and transformation.

Even if this appears to demand an historical approach, the analysis of citizenship through rights claiming, practice, and actions has seldom been applied to the past.[37] Such analyses of politics today fall short of their own aims in treating citizenship as open and contestable if they do not challenge the 'given-ness' of the contemporary state to which citizens belong. In this case, it requires recognition that any polity's own claims to legitimacy involves the erasure of its alternatives. In large part, study of citizenship in former settler colonies with indigenous populations has done most to render colonialism a central concern in the study of citizenship.[38] The fractious and conflicting repertoires of political action available to the postcolonial citizen have also been well explored by a number of recent scholars.[39] Such accounts point to the deficiencies of historical accounts of citizenship that see state-building and thus modern citizenship as a matter of organizing relatively homogenous populations. The point then is to move beyond descriptions of fundamental inequalities between political subjects within a polity toward explanations of how the politics of this inequality operates.[40]

IV

The next chapter, and much of the rest of this book, will be concerned with illustrating aspects of this development with examples from the British and French empires in the nineteenth century. I will focus on four conceptual assumptions that underlie what is meant by imperial citizenship as an historical phenomenon. The first is the use of the term 'citizenship' when describing so many different historical contexts. Following on from that, the second recognizes the importance of studying gradations within and between categories, such as the difference between 'citizen' and 'subject'. Third, certain activities or conditions that have in different times and places indicated this membership of a polity. They are an essential aspect of the study of citizenship as something mutable and contested that is claimed or enacted as much as it is conferred. A crucial question here is the extent to which nationalist or anticolonial actions should be considered an aspect of the history of political belonging under empire. Finally, using historical examples from imperial citizenship, I will address the question of empire as a space or series of spaces in which imperial belonging is enacted. These four conceptual problems are central to an historical understanding of being a citizen in the contemporary world.

Looking at the four problems in more detail, first, the development of what eventually comes to be called citizenship is a key concern of this book. Citizenship is used here to describe something that encompasses more than context-specific historical instances of use of the word 'citizen' in political language.[41] Such a history would be entirely valid, and a central argument of this book is that citizenship and what it entails should not be seen as a persistent concept. In part, this is because ideological statements about citizenship are only a limited aspect of this inquiry. To a much greater extent, this is a history of interpretations and practices and the ways they have been shaped by geographical and historical variance.

The 'subject' or 'citizen' are not to be studied as fixed forms but as categories that are continually redeployed and reconstituted, and not always clearly distinct from each other. From the nineteenth century, France legally had both citizens and subjects. In many polities where the two statuses existed together such as in France, formal acquisition of citizenship by some groups within colonial populations was possible. Equally, at times certain groups were formally deprived of citizenship, such as the Jews in France under the Vichy regime. However, this narrowly legal reading belies many of the ambiguities about how these two categories were constituted in the past. A close historical contextualization of terms such as 'citizenship', 'national', and 'subject' points to a richer history than a narrow focus on the specificity of each term allows. As Hannah Weiss Muller observes in her account of the British Empire in the eighteenth century, 'viewing the subject as a kind of disenfranchised citizen overlooks the possibilities in the relationship between subject and monarch. Subjects persistently laid claim to economic, political and legal concessions and they powerfully expressed both deference and demands'.[42] The history of what is called citizenship is one that ranges across nominal statuses. As Muller notes, these categories remain contested. Moreover, much of this contestation is what constitutes the rights claiming and enactment of political belonging that we are concerned with. The question of how the word 'citizen' has been deployed and how it relates to other terms such as 'national' or 'subject' in French and British colonial contexts will be discussed in more detail in the next chapter. As Muller's work very ably demonstrates, even formal legal definitions of such statuses tell us little about how they were enacted. We are looking therefore at the history of types of action, such as claiming legal and political rights, rather than of the character of certain categories such as 'subject'. Consistent with the approach developed by contemporary critical citizenship studies, our interest is in a range of repertoires of action, of ways of being political. They share in common a relationship of belonging to a polity. The modern term 'citizenship' bears an historical legacy of these different types of political action. It is more than the mere history of the specific use of the term 'citizen' or its close equivalents in different contexts.

Second, the multiple contexts in which empire is politically constituted encourage an awareness of gradations and distinctions in formal conditions that are a pronounced feature of empire-states. One can see this in plural legal jurisdictions and also in the legal, political, and social negotiations of *gens de couleur* in places such as Haiti and Martinique during the eighteenth and nineteenth centuries. Another example is the *millet* system in the Ottoman Empire, which provided different legal rights to recognized groups or 'nations'.[43] This is not to say that group differentiated rights, meaning the conferral of different sets of rights or obligations to different groups within the same polity, or plural jurisdictions, have been absent from the history of nation-states, but rather that these should be treated as central objects of study. Much postcolonial writing on political belonging under colonialism has emphasized the abject, the non-citizen status. Certain group identities have been seen as reinforcing this. Race, ethnicity, sex, property ownership, conviction for certain crimes, having a certain mental capacity, among other criteria have all been used for withholding or conferring citizenship. Simply being of a particular state—subject to its protection and its laws—does not necessarily confer being part of the people who actively constitute the state. Moreover, noncitizens themselves have rarely been a homogenous group. Writing about late colonial Africa, Mahmood Mamdani argues that the hierarchization of different racial groups—with each receiving different levels of political access—was a key feature of exclusion from citizenship under empire.[44] Those who belong to the polity but are not its citizens are a crucial element of the history of citizenship precisely because this exclusion is never fixed and often defined in relation to the rights of other groups. This is a reason why citizenship has often been theorized as alterity.[45] The inequalities between and within colonial and non-colonial populations are an observable pattern but have little explanatory power.

Modern empires have frequently exhibited this pattern whereby the supposed single entity is comprised of various constitutional arrangements, realized to differing degrees across different spaces. In this sense, the popular idea of a metropole and a periphery, of France and its colonies for example, provides an attractively neat model for explaining the different legal spaces of empire. In a recent study of imperial citizenship in the modern Atlantic empire, Josep Fradera has described this as a tendency to the creation of special laws and regimes for the metropole. It persisted throughout the nineteenth and twentieth centuries, he argues, regardless of frequent efforts to create a genuinely universal category of imperial belonging.[46] Many French colonial subjects who set foot in mainland France actually enjoyed far greater civil rights than they would in their own colony. This was made formal from 1881 in the draconian *Code de l'indigénat*, a set of French colonial restrictions on the rights of native subjects in colonies as wide ranging as Senegal and Algeria. It differed significantly in its application across colonial contexts and did not apply to the same people when they were in France. Different types of colony witnessed different kinds of political claims-making and different forms of domination. In many contexts strict controls on migration and property ownership were often intended to limit heterogeneity. This can be seen, for example, in the severe restrictions on Europeans in the territories of British India under East India Company rule in the first half of the nineteenth century. However, even an acknowledgment of the types of polity that intermingled within single empires ignores the patchy way in which the granting and deprivation of rights were constituted within supposedly homogenous spaces. Rules pertaining to a single territory were often more or less constituted only in certain parts—urban centers or trade routes for example. This has been shown in the work of Lauren Benton on how the acting out of sovereignty was uneven. Rather than being spread evenly and exclusively within contiguous territories, it could spread unevenly along networks of commerce, travel, and military occupation.[47]

The possibility of inclusion for nominally excluded or excludable groups has been a significant element of the organization of colonial rule, certainly in the examples covered here of the British and

French empires in the nineteenth century. As Isin observes, the rise of correctional sites as technologies of citizenship, 'such as hospitals, workhouses, prisons, schools, housing projects, and other institutions, marked the characteristic form of disciplinary professionalization [. . .] what made these strategies and technologies of citizenship different [. . .] was that citizenship was constituted as an attainable goal for strangers and outsiders, rather than an unattainable ideal'.[48] What should concern us here is not the feasibility of such aspirations but their function in articulating political actions. This foregrounds important fields of study. The aspirational and negotiated aspects of political life under empire have been considered in works such as Bayly's explorations of the intellectual history of liberalism in British India.[49] Equally, de facto inequality and oppression can be contrasted with formal or superficial claims to equality of belonging, as has been shown in Sukanya Banerjee's study of British India, *Becoming Imperial Citizens*. Nominal legal protection was often rendered inconsequential in the face of race-based formal restrictions or practices.[50] In all these examples, the idea of attainable political belonging for colonial subjects has been a significant feature of the rhetoric and form of colonial rule. The range of different formal statuses and the fluidity of their meaning within the imperial polity are a justification for the move beyond a dyad of exclusion and inclusion; citizen and noncitizen; colonizer and colonized. As Étienne Balibar has noted, 'We cannot be content simply to reiterate the sort of generic discourse on inclusion and exclusion, inside and outside, belonging and nonbelonging that underlies the invocation of a "community of citizens" '.[51] This is no less the case when we talk about colonial subjects.

Third, if we understand the historical formation of citizenship not simply as a conferred status but as a repertoire of actions, how do acts of resistance and revolution relate to imperial citizenship? The apparent rupture or promise of rupture of the status quo that anticolonial movements have appeared to offer can lead to a downplaying or reframing of political actions that articulated themselves within the imperial polity.[52] As Mimi Sheller demonstrates in her comparison of independent Haiti and British-rule Jamaica in the mid-nineteenth century, freedom was not absolute. The education system and parish structure of Jamaica did more in this period to foster civil society than the elite-controlled military dictatorship of Haiti.[53] Moreover, resistance as a form of rights claiming was not always articulated as nationalist or more than reformist. I make these observations not to somehow vindicate colonial enterprise but rather to indicate analytical frames of reference for understanding the history of citizenship in empire.

Whether resistance is described merely as protest or as emergent or actual nationalism, it is a key political action under imperial rule.[54] The right to resist or at least the historical legitimacy of resistance has been central to the idea of what it is to be a citizen in many countries. This includes imperial powers such as France and the United States. As will be seen, this aspect of 'western' traditions of citizenship has also been a feature of some anticolonial movements. To pick one example, as Paul Gilroy notes, 'The world becomes a different place once the history of black resistance in the western hemisphere has been added to our understanding of it'.[55] This is relevant for the study of imperial citizenship, because it reminds us that resistance as a mechanism for expanding the scope of what citizenship is, and who can be a citizen, has been a common feature of the debate about what it actually means to be a citizen. However, if legitimate political expression among the colonized is reduced to violent resistance alone, we exclude the radical possibilities of other forms of rights-claims.[56] Such an approach might be seen to be too willing to accommodate resistance within that which it resists, to incorporate the anticolonial into the colonial. Similar objections have, as we have seen, been made to the way critical citizenship studies might articulate resistance to the authority of the state as a form of belonging within that polity. My point here echoes that of Gilroy. The history of empire's legacy for contemporary political forms such as citizenship must include the role of resistance to it.

I turn now to the question of addressing empire as a polity. Inconsistent, transient spatial concentrations of power are a key feature of the operation of colonial rule.[57] Rapid transfers of formal sovereignty over colonial populations were a feature of nineteenth-century European empires. Hannah Weiss Muller has described the varied Catholic populations that found themselves under British rule in Canada, the Caribbean, and the Mediterranean, enjoying political and civil freedoms that their coreligionists in Britain did not have.[58] The British Empire in the nineteenth century encompassed multiple legal systems that incorporated elements of practice from previous ruling powers such as the Spanish in Trinidad and Tobago, the Mughals and their successor regimes in much of India and the French in parts of Canada, all of which were part of the same British Empire. Immense geographical variation in the interpretation of subjecthood and its implications was a characteristic of political and civic belonging under empire. A common way of rendering this has been to divide imperial space into a metropole and a periphery—a center where the 'colonizers' are based and the place they colonize. The two may be legally distinct places. They may have different majority populations. Metropolitans (or their racially identifiable descendants) may have superior rights to the local inhabitants when in the periphery. Such a model for the understanding of imperial space fails to fully account for the piecemeal and negotiated nature of the polities it composed.[59] Lauren Benton ably describes the complex patterns that are often at play in her study of sovereignty in the modern era. For Benton, the notional uniformity of a sovereign space belies the extent to which the exercise of powers follows different patterns, based for example along routes of trade and defense or constituted at certain points along a border.[60] As Edward Whiting Fox has explained about the historical geography of French colonial expansion in the early modern period, steadily growing settler populations were not essential. A sizable group of settlers in a territory could readily be substituted by 'an active exchange of goods and messages as well as a highly developed sense of common purpose'.[61] Scholars such as Benton invite us to begin with an understanding of networks for the transmission of people, knowledge, and goods and use it to understand the formations of laws and norms that accompanies them. Political and legal claims about absolute distinctions between one territory of an empire and another are significant in understanding the operation of political belonging. However, in and of themselves they fail to capture the complex spatial patterns of the exercise of that power, patterns that do not neatly equate with formal borders.[62] In this sense, formal territorial claims matter less than the patterns and networks of rights-claiming practices.[63]

These four assumptions are not distinct to the study of the historical formation through colonial rule of what comes to be called citizenship. Rather, a focus on the empire-state as opposed to the nation-state necessarily emphasizes important aspects of the history of citizenship, namely the limitations and value of using the term citizenship at all; the importance of recognizing distinctions and gradations within and between formal categories of political belonging that play out in the way they are practiced; the importance of what actions constitute being a citizen; and the role of multiple interacting spatial contexts in determining what constitutes citizenship.

V

This chapter has argued for an expansion of our understanding of the historical formation of citizenship. This is meant in two closely connected ways. First, it calls for an historical account of those actions and practices that we now include under the category of citizenship. Second, it argues that such a history of citizenship in western nation-states such as France and Britain would need to account for the effects of rule over colonial populations. A history of citizenship that incorporates that of empire- and nation-states does not present new repertoires of political action but may suggest new emphases and patterns, both for our understanding of the historical formation of citizenship of nation-states and of the colonial past. The history of citizenship in an empire-state, as in any polity, recounts the development of rights, obligations, capacities, and types of action that often come to be viewed retrospectively as citizenship. It is also the history of a normative concept. Both aspects of the history of citizenship are essential to our understanding of how empire-states have created many of the features of contemporary citizenship.

To search for the history of aspects of political belonging in imperial citizenship is not to underplay empire as domination. Colonial violence as an aspect of governance and anticolonial protest as a rejection of the colonial state both raise challenges to our understanding of the relationship between that state and its colonial subjects. The question of how these can be incorporated into an account of the life of a polity is one that contemporary citizenship studies grapples with when addressing issues such as the deprivation of citizenship, police brutality, the erosion of rights, and violent responses from the citizenry. The value of framing such investigations in terms of rights claiming is to provide a lens for determining how political action in a polity takes place.

As the next chapter will show, such a reading shifts the spatial location of western history away from the metropolitan centers of empire such as London and Paris. It renders empire and imperial domination integral to any understanding of the various rights, obligations, practices, and actions that comprise the idea of western citizenship. In this reading, colonial contexts did not simply receive or resist western political concepts and practices—they formed them.

Chapter 2

Freedom of the Press, Liberalism and the 'Garrison-State' in British India

I

Freedom of the press was one of the key rights associated with the rise of the liberal nation-state in the late eighteenth and early nineteenth centuries. As such, it is a key aspect of the historical formation of the liberal ideal of citizenship. In Britain, freedom of the press was a major rallying point for Whigs and radicals in the era of the Napoleonic Wars and the decade after.[1] This chapter charts governmental responses to claims for freedom of the press in British India between 1799, when censorship was imposed, and 1835, when restrictions were repealed. As in Britain, advocates for press freedom in British India questioned the legality of restrictions under English law. They feared that the unchecked executive power of the government might compromise the liberty of British subjects and they argued for the existence of a public capable of exercising that scrutiny. The key differences between Britain and British India that commentators observed lay in the recognition that the British were foreign imperial occupiers of India. There was the question of who the public was who held the British government in India to account, and the related matter of whether freedom of the press was desirable or even practicable without representative government. Restrictions on freedom of the press were resisted by both Europeans and Indians who did so by claiming rights as British subjects. The ways in which the language of liberty and authority could be fully transposed from its British to its Indian context reminds us that the administration of British India was not an exception to or aberration from the dominant registers of Anglophone liberalism (even if the attempts to deny its applicability clearly were).[2] Sharp divisions in the enjoyment of rights determined by race and religion that formed later in the century appear in this context harder to define consistently. The struggle between the authorities, Indian and European newspaper editors, and the law courts revealed tensions between the supposed rights of the British subject and the freedoms permitted under imperial government. It did so in ways that subverted as much as they reaffirmed the formal divisions made between 'Indians' and 'Europeans'.

Using the example of the English language press, which continues to play a central role in contemporary political life in India, this chapter attempts to show the ways in which British India was not so much a periphery or an exception but a center for the historical development of a major right associated with anglophone liberal thought. The claiming of press freedom in the context of imperial rule and the absence of representative government, undermines the teleological vision of the freedom of press as a right historically contingent upon the slow growth of democratic institutions in the west. As earlier chapters have argued, such histories are difficult to discern. In part, this is because to trace such evidence of political and civic life under subjugation has often been seen as a downplaying of colonial violence.[3] This chapter's analysis of the debates on press restrictions in British India between 1799 and their repeal in 1835 integrates four linked historiographical debates: liberalism and exclusion under imperial rule; notions of hybrid political and legal frameworks; the operation of the militaristic imperial state; and the inadequacy of theoretical frameworks regarding the political subject derived from western history.

First, it provides an analysis of the tension between law, executive power, and the public sphere under imperial rule that complements recent scholarship on nineteenth-century India as a site of liberal rights claiming. Studies looking at canonical political thinkers in the metropole have emphasized the apparent paradox of a British liberalism that bestowed rights at home, while denying them in the empire.[4] In some respects this seeming contradiction arises from the rather loose use of the term liberalism to encompass on the one hand the persistence of a civic republican concern with virtue, independence, and corruption (a trend that has long been acknowledged in the study of the Atlantic world), and on the other the utilitarian reforms of the 1820s onward.[5] A more nuanced understanding of the operation of 'western' political thought in the Indian context is now provided by an ever growing body of studies that look instead at the politics of day-to-day administration and a wider range of political participation beyond protest and resistance. In many cases, such work restores Indians to the history of liberalism in India, at the same time as casting light on the complex nexus of institutions and social groups that constituted imperial discourse.[6] These studies have shown how major figures such as Ram Mohan Roy invoked both their rights as British subjects and historic rights derived from the Mughal Empire in order to claim privileges and protections comparable to those afforded subjects of the metropole in areas such as freedom of the press. My study complements this perspective by detailing how government discourse interpreted these claims. In doing so, it reveals a self-reflexive debate about how and why liberty and authority should be constituted differently between colony and metropole. For example, the unwillingness to recognize a non-European public for the English-language press is an obvious aspect of the case against press freedom. However, until 1824, the government's powers to punish breaches of press restrictions with banishment could apply only to Europeans, enabling non-Europeans and mixed-race editors and proprietors to operate with greater freedom.[7] As the radical pamphleteer Colonel Stanhope observed, 'The Native could exercise his pen freely, though the European could not; for the Native, though nominally under the control of a Censor; could not, like the European, be banished at the will of the Governor-General in Council. Thus the Native was amenable to the law alone, but the European writer was subjected to no defined law, but to the arbitrary will of a Censor'.[8] Freedom of the press, as with other debates about the application of English law, shows that the problem of who enjoyed the rights of a British subject was complex and mutable in both its resolution and its consequences.[9] The anomalous legal freedoms given to Indians under English law and denied to Europeans by the government's restrictions remind us that the reconstitution of colonized peoples as inferior subjects under the law was a haphazard and uneven process and these qualities stemmed from tensions within the colonial legal regime itself.[10]

Secondly, my argument here benefits from studies that have demonstrated the decentered way in which imperial power was constituted and experienced through a nexus of institutions. Just as it would be a fallacy to see British legal thought in this period as a coherent and consistent whole, the same is equally true of imperial law with its multiple jurisdictions and differing mixes of pluralism.[11] As Jon Wilson emphasizes, India, like other colonial settings, was actually a place where many 'western concepts' were effectively constituted. It was not simply a passive receiver of something pre-built elsewhere.[12] For these reasons, this chapter suggests that the claims about the hybridity of British legal discourse in an imperial Indian setting, made so well by Robert Travers, require us to avoid assuming that this pattern is discernible to the same extent in freedom of the press.[13] Property, and its manifestation in the administration of justice and revenue, has been studied disproportionately to other discourses of governmentality in British India. In contrast to these fields, freedom of the press is an example of a debate in which the precedent of Indian practices played a relatively marginal role in the articulation of rights in spite of the frequency with which it was invoked. Broadly, this is because while there were some examples of press regulation from Mughal administration, the law was ultimately derived from British legal practice. Moreover, the combination of new printing technology, new forms of political discourse, and rapid imperial consolidation of domestic government meant that there were few significant precedents.

Thirdly, current interest in how liberties were claimed and withheld in empire should not be seen as a departure from a previous historiographical emphasis on militarism as the dominant mode of British imperial government in the early nineteenth century.[14] Indeed, the two historiographical strands should be better integrated. On the one hand the opposition to freedom of the press provides a fuller articulation of the romantic conservatism associated with the dominant ideologues of company rule in the 1820s, Sir John Malcolm and Sir Thomas Munro.[15] On the other, the ways in which the courts in the three presidencies of Bengal, Madras (now Chennai), and Bombay (now Mumbai) were used to counteract the authoritarianism of their governments provide an interesting corrective to any notion of an all-pervasive garrison-state of the East India Company. As Peers has argued, military-fiscalism placed economic and ideological constraints on the reforming administration of William Cavendish Bentinck from 1828 to 1835.[16] Legal developments, such as the campaign for freedom of the press, suggest a more nuanced story, one that gives greater agency to nongovernmental elites (both Indian and European), at the same time as foregrounding the tension between executive power and the application of law. Partha Chatterjee is right to observe that the overall context for the debates over freedom of the press in British India was one of subjugation of a colonized population. However, this in itself tells us little about the practice of civic life under empire. The manifestation of rights claiming under empire is an important counterweight to a narrowly 'western' narrative of such trends precisely because of the context of militarism and authoritarianism in which it takes place.[17]

Following from this, the Indian side of the debate about freedom of the press also exposes the inadequacy of theoretical frameworks regarding the political subject derived from western history. There is an entire discourse of rights claiming related to freedom of the press, which was not in origin contingent on rights claiming regarding representative government. The issue is less the way certain non-European political trajectories are discounted or entirely ignored. Rather, it is the neglect of the role of non-European contexts in the historical formation of these 'western' discourses. When we consider that English-language newspapers only ceased to be the most popular in India in 1978, it is clear that the Indian context for this major right in anglophone liberal thought has been massively neglected or misinterpreted.[18] For our present purposes, the main problems of applying mainstream 'western' frameworks to India are first the issue of a 'split public' and secondly the relationship of freedom of the press to other rights. Of the many critiques of Habermas's public sphere in a colonial context, the most relevant is the idea of a 'split public . . . in which an internal social division is accompanied by an ideological division that justifies the divide while claiming to overcome it'.[19] While Rajagopal's emphasis here is on the cultural and religious heterogeneity that colonial governments extenuated and exploited, it is easy to overlook the fact that before 1857, European subjects also formed part of this split public of the governed. Moreover, the case of the European public and the question of its rights reveals the strains created by a legally pluralistic colonial regime. Aside from this, it is certainly true that Habermas's account of the public sphere in Germany in the same period provides a useful understanding of press restrictions under authoritarian government (particularly, as will be seen later, on the primary role of bureaucracies as opposed to executive government in censorship).[20] Equally, most of the advocates of a free press invoked precisely the same narratives of progress, derived from European history, as their counterparts in Britain. For example, as Colonel Stanhope observed, 'History teaches, that a reformation in the religion of the Hindoos could not be effected by the intolerant Mahomedan; nor by the Inquisition, with its synods and censors, and their impious decrees; nor even by the preaching of pious missionaries.

It cannot fail, however, to be produced, as in Europe, by the influence of free discussion'.[21] Nevertheless, an insurmountable weakness in applying Habermas's framework to British India is the fact that press freedom is associated with the rise of representative government in his account. This is a fault inherent to the sources he used and the implicit teleology of an historical narrative constructed to explain contemporary Western Europe. As will be seen, one of the major points of interest about the Indian debate is the widespread assumption that freedom of press was only necessary or appropriate where the government was accountable to the people as its representative.

This chapter examines how the various groups that constituted the government of British India understood freedom of the press as a right and what this reveals about their conception of the imperial state there. Drawing on the extensive East India Company records, published Parliamentary Papers and numerous pamphlets produced on the topic, it attempts to provide an alternative and complementary emphasis to previous detailed studies by Bayly and Zastoupil that have looked at the editors themselves, particularly James Silk Buckingham and Ram Mohan Roy. It goes on to describe the major regulations that were enacted in this period in the context of precedents from the government of Britain and British India. The issue of the roles played by Europeans and Indians in claiming the right to hold government to account will then be discussed. By way of conclusion, press regulation will be put into the broader context of the clash between militarism and reform that characterized the intellectual history of the East India Company administration of India in the 1820s and 1830s. Freedom of the press will be used as an example of how the idea of a split between liberalism at home and despotism abroad must be modified to account for the liberal rights claiming of British imperial subjects in India.

II

Before discussing the changing regulation regime between 1799 and 1835, it is worth tracing the main assumptions that informed the debate in the contexts of Britain and British India. While Indian precedents were claimed to a limited degree, overwhelmingly this was a debate about the conferring of rights given to British subjects under English law. In Britain, freedom of the press was historically linked to the protection of the liberty of the people and the concomitant need for scrutiny of the Parliament. In its Indian context, as we will see, another dimension emerged, the tension between the legal powers of the Governor General in Council to enforce their regulations upon British subjects and the protections those subjects enjoyed under English law.

Three aspects of the freedom of the press in British history are significant for understanding its British Indian context: the historically constituted liberty of British subjects; the need to hold government to the account of the public; and the radical call to expand the public. First, it was recognized by its promoters and their opponents as a historic right in English law. The key historic text used in this period to sanction freedom of the press was John Milton's *Areopagitica* (1644), which declared that 'the state shall be my governors but not my critics'. It was invoked by both those opposed to all press regulations and their opponents, including the Legal Counsel of the East India Company in 1822. He began by noting, 'The Interference of the Governing power in the relation to the Press has always been exercised in all States: in free States to a less degree than in despotic States such as Indian to an illimitable degree'. He then proceeded to quote from Milton: 'I deny not, but that it is of greatest concernment in the Church and Commonwealth, to have a vigilant eye on how Books demean themselves as well as men; and thereafter to confine, imprison, and do sharpest justice on them as malefactors'.[22] As in Britain, government repression of rights, embodied in the Six Acts of 1819, was not a denial of their existence rather than an entreaty for greater security.[23] Secondly, its key function was the scrutiny of government. In 1762, the radical John Wilkes had described it as 'the terror of all bad ministers; for their dark and dangerous designs, or their weakness, inability, and duplicity, have this been detected and shown to the public generally'.[24] Throughout the eighteenth century, the focus of this call for greater scrutiny had been the right to freely and fully report debates in Parliament. Indeed, Hansard, which records all proceedings in Parliament, was established by the radical William Cobbett in 1802. As another radical, James Mill, observed in *Liberty of the Press* in 1820, 'It is doubtful whether a power in the people of choosing their own rulers, without the liberty of the press, would be an advantage'.[25] In other words, the campaign for liberty of the press was conceptually linked to the historic growth of representative government in Britain. As the Court of Directors of the East India Company argued, 'Wherever a government emanates from the people and is responsible to them, the people must necessarily have the privilege of discussing the measures of Government. . . . But in no sense of the terms can the Government of India be called a free, a representative or a popular Government'.[26] Thirdly, for the radicals, freedom of the press was intimately associated with increasing the public awareness of the common reader. It was therefore intended to expand the public, meaning in this context those capable of taking an interest in public affairs and holding the government to account. As will be seen a little later, the main advocates of press freedom, such as James Silk Buckingham, pushed for a broader radical agenda that included promoting European colonization and Western learning.[27]

The first regulations appeared in 1799 under the administration of Richard Wellesley and were consistent with the thickening of the military-fiscal state that characterized his rule. The five rules were:

> 1stly Every printer of a Newspaper to print his name at the Bottom of the Paper; 2ndly Every editor and proprietor of a paper to deliver in his name and place of abode to the Secretary of the Government; 3rdly No paper to be published on a Sunday; 4thly No paper to be published at all until it shall have been previously inspected by the Secretary to the Government or by a person authorized by him for that purpose; 5thly The penalty for offending against any of the above regulations to be immediate embarkation to Europe.[28]

The first rule reflects a desire to monitor and control the printing process itself (a trend that would persist and increase long after the repeal of 1835). The second rule recognized that, as in Britain, the growth of the radical press in the 1790s brought with it the rise of the editor or proprietor (often the same person rather than the individual author) as a distinct actor in the growth of the revolutionary press.[29] Restrictions on the Sabbath were entirely consistent with Wellesley's efforts to reinforce the Christian character of Europeans in India.[30] This was a backlash against the assimilation of local custom and syncretism of the 1770s and 1780s and the moral and social equality with native populations it implied. The fourth rule imposed censorship. Infractions of this clause included both the failure to submit copy to the censor before production and neglecting to follow all the censor's instructions. The fifth point would ultimately cause the most political problems. Significantly, it was a power the government held only over individuals who resided in its territories subject to its license (a category synonymous with 'Europeans' in writings of the time).³¹

The regulations were a part of the antirevolutionary authoritarianism of the French wars of the 1790s, but only inasmuch as they were part of an attempt to centralize and control knowledge gathering and circulation by Wellesley's administration.³² Contemporary with the regulations, Wellesley initiated the *Government Gazette*, a private newspaper that would be the main channel for public information from the government. The Gazette was to 'contain such articles of public notification as the Governor General may think proper to direct and may be accompanied by a Newspaper containing articles of intelligence and private advertisements to be published under the inspection and control of the Chief Secretary but not to be considered like the Gazette as an Official communication'.³³ There was no ambiguity about the greater purpose of the Gazette: 'In a political view, a powerful motive arises in favour of the proposed Establishment. The increase of private printing presses in India, unlicensed however controlled is an evil of the first magnitude in its consequences. Of this sufficient proof is to be found in the scandalous outrages from the year 1793 to 1798'.³⁴ It was hoped that 'the Establishment of a press by the Supreme Government would effectively silence those which now exist and would as certainly prevent the establishment of such in the future'.³⁵ In other words, the plan recognized government information as the source of the newspapers' power. The major cases of breach of the censorship rules in this period reveal a concern over military security. The implementation of the censorship rules and relevant regulations also expose a mutable distinction between political and non-political matters. The discretion to define the political enabled the government to introduce further control on the press. Thus, in 1813, censorship of advertisements was introduced. It is worth noting that advertising income provided papers with a financial independence that translated into editorial freedom.³⁶ In general terms, breaches of the censorship rules were less severely enforced under subsequent Governors General.³⁷

In 1818, censorship in Bengal was revoked and replaced by a set of regulations which editors were obliged to follow. As before, banishment was the only punishment the government was able to enforce (and then, only on Europeans).[38] The regulations prohibited the following:

1. Animadversions on the measures and proceedings of the honorable court of directors, or other public authorities in England, connected with the government in India; or disquisitions on political transactions of the local administration.
2. Discussions having a tendency to create alarm or suspicion among the native population of any intended interference with their religious opinions.
3. The republication, from English or other newspapers, of passages coming under any of the above heads, or otherwise calculated to affect the British power or reputation in India.
4. Private scandal and personal remarks on individuals, tending to excite dissension in society.[39]

The regulations soon caused tension in Madras, where the government continued to operate censorship. A public meeting praised the governor general, the Marquis of Hastings, and invited him to intervene. As one speaker, George Stavely, a local lawyer, declared, 'I know of no law, there is none upon your Statute Book, which restrains the Liberty of the Indian Press; I speak in the hearing of those who will correct me if I am wrong'.[40] The ensuing battle between the governor of Madras and the press soon soured. The governor wrote in a minute to the Court of Directors in 1820, 'I have been subjected to much scurrility and personal abuse in the public prints, which have found protection and encouragement at Calcutta. . . . Their principal objects have been to disseminate the worst political doctrines of the times, to bring the constituted authorities both in European and in Asia into contempt, to spread feuds in private society, and to provide profit for Lawyers form prosecutions of libels in the Courts of Justice'.[41] Madras would retain censorship, but as will be seen, the consequences in terms of the inconsistent application of regulations across the presidencies and the ensuing political scandal would ultimately lead to the end of press regulations.

The most famous scandal regarding freedom of the press erupted soon after when the editor of the *Calcutta Journal*, James Silk Buckingham, was banished. The details of the case, which became a *cause célèbre* among British radicals, are well described in the voluminous official correspondence generated by the Parliamentary Inquiry of 1834. There is little to add to the recent accounts of Buckingham and the freedom of the press provided by Bayly and Zastoupil. Of interest is the way that the Buckingham case elevated freedom of the press to a central issue for the authorities back in Britain and for the ways in which, as we will see, it encouraged all parties to articulate their position on the role a free press would have in an imperial context such as British India. Parallel events in London and Calcutta (presently Kolkata) now led to the introduction of a stricter set of regulations. The Court of Directors disapproved of the regulations as soon as they received news of them. Canning, president of the Board of Control (the government body that supervised the Company), shared their unease but refused to allow the regulations to be revoked. Canning's motives reveal a great deal about the self-reflexive nature of the debate: freedom of the press had once again become a significant issue in England, and he knew that Parliament would disapprove of a move to maintain censorship.[42] Instead, at a secret meeting in March 1823, it was resolved that the new governor general, Lord Amherst, would be authorized by the Board and the Court to impose and enforce more stringent regulations.[43] The Company's defense of its actions in the 1834 select committee cited the secret meeting as the legal sanction for the imposition of restricted measures, arguing that Canning, as president of the Board of Control, had the deferred authority of Parliament to intervene in an area where 'the law of England is silent' and 'where the ends of good order and civil government' require it.[44]

In 1823, a new set of regulations was introduced. The differences between the regulations were carefully analyzed by the Supreme Court judges at the time. The new regulations undoubtedly gave more control to the government, yet they also provided clarity. The picture that emerged was more consistent with the twin obsessions of the militarists such as Malcolm and Munro of protecting 'traditional society' and guarding against internal and external unrest. The second rule on the creation of alarm within the native population was now more specific, with the addition of a prohibition on 'irritating and insulting remarks on their peculiar usages and modes of thinking on . . . religious subjects'.[45] Articles of this type had appeared regularly in the censor's office and reflected the divergence between orientalists and Anglicists of the 1820s and 1830s.[46] The third rule's restriction on reporting on the operations of the various government bodies now included the policies of the native states. Many of the rules were clearly intended to curb the frequency of libel actions, inasmuch as they sought to reduce censure of the government. Hence, the eighth rule prohibited 'Anonymous appeals to the Public relative to grievances alleged to have been sustained by public Officers in the Service of His Majesty or the Honourable Company'. The fourth rule of 1818 banned 'Private Scandal and personal remarks on Individuals tending to excite discussion in Society'. The seventh rule forbade only 'Defamatory publications tending to distract the peace harmony and good order of society'.[47] Advocate General Robert Spankie commented that 'the general provisions are very properly adapted from Acts of Parliament for the suppression of mischiefs somewhat similar to those against which this measure is directed though cases exactly alike cannot be expected to have occurred at home'.[48] This basis in Acts of Parliament was a vital condition.

To be enforceable, the regulations needed to be registered by the Supreme Courts in the three presidencies. While the court in Bengal registered the regulations, that of Bombay did not. In 1826, its chief justice, Sir Edward West, ruled, 'In my opinion, if there be an authority to pass this regulation, there is a general authority to turn any act into a misdemeanor, triable by Justices of the Peace, and thus at once to do away with the trial by jury, and oust the jurisdiction of this Court'.[49] West was clear too that even in Bengal, the regulations could only apply to the printing of newspapers by 'English subjects' in Calcutta. After several attempts, the failure in Madras led the government to give up on registering the regulations. The government's solicitor stated, 'I humbly recommend that the matter should not be pressed; and I feel satisfied that the present Judges of the Supreme Court will be ready to do what may be required to preserve the peace, harmony and good order of society, should any circumstances hereafter arise to render such a Regulation necessary at this presidency'.[50] In all cases, the issue turned on whether there was a sufficient threat to the peace to justify such restrictions. This reminds us that as a legal issue, it was essentially about the application of English law in specific jurisdictions to maintain order. As in its metropolitan context, in British India, it was rendered as a problem of the authority of government and the liberty of the subject.[51]

The reformism of the 1830s led to a *de facto* and finally a *de jure* repeal of the regulations. With the arrival of Governor General Bentinck in 1827, the relative freedom enjoyed by editors in Bombay and Madras was matched by a reluctance to enforce the regulations in Bengal. The government's stance in Bengal reflected the general mood among local elites, as shown by a series of public meetings held in January and June 1835, which led to the petitioning of government. At the January meeting, a resolution was passed which noted, 'The British government was more honoured by the natives now than ever it was under those who had introduced these restrictions'.[52] Thomas Babington Macaulay, as Law Member of the Council, was asked to coordinate the repeal of the legislation. Noting the discrepancy between the letter of the law and its enforcement, he observed, 'The newspapers have for years been allowed as ample a measure of practical liberty as that which they enjoy in England'. Using the language of liberty that was such a strong feature of all previous discussions, he observed, 'The very words "license to print" have a sound hateful to the ears of Englishmen in every part of the globe'.[53] To the argument that such laws were required for a possible emergency, Macaulay responded by noting the considerable powers available to the governor general, both acting alone and in Council: 'Possessing as we do the unquestionable power to interfere, whenever the safety of the State may require it, with overwhelming rapidity and entry, we surely are not, in quiet times, to be constantly keeping the office and ceremony form of despotism before the eyes of those whom, nevertheless we permit to enjoy the substance of freedom'.[54] Whereas the 1799 regulations had invoked the greater control of the state, and the 1823 regulations had stressed the need for security, the 1835 repeal embodied the liberalism of the 1830s.

III

Having reviewed the major changes in regulations, it is now necessary to consider the complex question of why freedom of the press was seen to be necessary or appropriate. All sides shared a presumption that the press existed to serve a public and to inform public opinion. The question that was asked at the time was whether such a public existed in India. Did European residents in India constitute a public? If so, surely servants of the East India Company or its army could not be considered part of this public. A more complex question was whether an Indian public existed for the English language press. What follows is a discussion of how both the Indian public and the European public in India were conceived in the free press debate. This distinction allows us to understand how press freedom was associated with the need for a body of rights bearing subjects to hold their government to account in the context of the British Empire in India (as opposed to metropolitan Britain).

The question of whether a European public existed in India was approached directly. Just as Buckingham's *Calcutta Journal* had addressed itself to an English-speaking public in India, his great opponent in the government of Bengal, John Adam, vehemently denied that such a public existed. In a memorandum of October 1822, he listed those who would make up the European public in India: Company servants, merchants, and the 'lower class of men of business, traders and handicraftsmen'.[55] The memorandum concluded, 'It is a mockery to dignify such a community with the name of Public, and to claim for it the potential privileges and functions of the great and independent body of the People of England'. As Adam wrote, 'Whilst I acknowledge this right of holding public officers to account, I protest against the assumption of this right of control over the Indian Government and its Officers by a community constituted of the European Society of these Presidencies'.[56] Concerns about the civic qualities of the European population of British India had been a common theme in the run up to the 1813 East India Act (which gave greater access and mobility to European private citizens).[57] The dangers to the state of treating such people as participants in political life would later be affirmed by the two great ideologues of East India Company rule in this period: Sir John Malcolm and Sir Thomas Munro.[58]

Those who denied the existence of a public in India to hold government to account often argued that such a public ultimately existed in England as the Company had delegated authority from Parliament.[59] The Court of Directors' statement on this is worth quoting at length for its reference to the structures of power that were seen to make despotic government of Indians by a free people constitutionally sustainable without endangering the liberty of the latter or inflicting tyranny on the former:

> The regulations of the Indian government under which Taxes are levied and justice is administered are not only promulgated in India but are regularly sent home and laid before Parliament. Every communication which takes place in India upon every public measure is placed upon record and complete diaries of the proceedings of the local Government in every

department of Administration being annually transmitted to the Court of Directors the fullest information respecting these proceedings as well as the proceedings at home to which they gave rise are at all times accessible to the Public of their Country through their Representatives in Parliament and the Indian Government this becomes amenable in the last resort to a Public far more enlightened then the Indian Public and accustomed by the enjoyment of popular rights to view with exceeding jealousy measures originating in absolute power.[60]

There was a wider issue. As Buckingham would remark: 'The hypocritical profession of deference to public opinion in England, to the exclusion of public opinion in India, is a mere pretence held out to entrap the unwary, and to induce men to believe that the objection is merely to the class of people who are to exercise this scrutiny'.[61] He went on, 'If the constitutional control of public opinion be really vested in the great body of the people—as the Governor General admits it is in England—are not the British inhabitants of India, so far as they extend, as much an integral part of the "great body of the people" when residing on the banks of the Ganges, as they would be if dwelling on the banks of the Thames?'[62] For opponents such as Sir John Malcolm, imperial occupation of India made it appropriate to 'assimilate with the national government of England the unnational government which extraordinary events have given us in India'.[63] As Malcolm remarked on the debate over the Buckingham case, 'It is no easy task to reconcile Englishmen to any principles which have an appearance of militating against that freedom, to which, from their very birth, they are so fondly attached; but they will not refuse assent to the reasonableness of some departure from these principles, if proved to be alike essential to maintain the prosperity and glory of their country, and to promote the good and tranquility of distant nations, who, though subject to its power, are, and must long continue, in a totally different state of society'.[64] This was consistent with the legal justification for the regulations on grounds of order, but it also made a further claim, that such rights could never be fully enjoyed in an empire such as British India. As Macaulay's minute in 1835 makes clear, regardless of the question of what rights Indians should enjoy, one indissoluble issue remained: reason of state could only provide a temporary and unsatisfactory justification for curtailing the rights of British subjects under the jurisdiction of English law.

An Indian public was said to exist both in the recent history of Mughal and other native courts and through the tiny but growing number of elite Indians who had access to English-speaking newspapers. Many proponents of a free press invoked Indian precedent. They pointed to the general toleration of Emperor Akbar's court and to the existence of court newsletters. As the radical free press campaigner Stanhope said, 'The historians of Indostan wrote with freedom on the conduct and duties of their sovereigns, and some of their rulers acted up to the noble principles which their Chroniclers inculcated. . . . Persons are apt to make a boastful contrast between British rule and the system of anarchy that preceded it. Let them rather compare the noble administration of Akbar with that even of a Cornwallis or a Hastings'.[65] This had two significances. First, the Indian precedent was designed to show that a free press was consistent with a South Asian despotism. Secondly, it also suggested the presence of an Indian public, of members of the community engaged in discussion about political life. It is worth saying that unlike in revenue administration for example, this precedent was not used to adapt press regulations to any supposed 'Indian norms'. Rather, it was invoked as an argument for allowing comparable freedoms to those enjoyed in Great Britain. Opponents were quick to deny the comparisons between Indian practices and a free press. As John Malcolm wrote, 'At the courts of most of the native princes, papers of news, termed Ackbars, are produced; which are court-gazettes, giving a statement of occurrences, true or false, as matters of fact, without comment or opinion. From the situation of the writers under such governments, it will easily be conceived that these Ackbars bear no affinity to an English newspaper'.[66] As the petition of 1835 suggests, the question of whether an Indian public was seen to exist is of interest because its defenders saw this as a right that belonged to all subjects of British rule.

The freedom of the press debate appeared at a significant conjuncture in Indian intellectual history and this is reflected in the ways in which the presence of an Indian public was discussed. As Wilson and Bayly have argued, Ram Mohan Roy and other members of the Bengal elite should be seen as part of a colonial Indian tradition of liberalism that was not essentially different in its vocabulary from 'western' liberal thought.[67] One can take this argument even further in the case of freedom of the press, because the right to freedom of the press was invoked by Indians as a right they enjoyed as British subjects. The resolution of the January 1835 public meeting petitioning for a free press stated that Europeans had 'a common cause with the natives'. It went on to say there was 'no principle that should make them dangerous, which would not make Englishmen danger. If the government be a liberal and enlightened one, and the power were given feely to resent their grievances, they would all support the British supremacy'.[68] The records of the meeting note that this statement was greeted with support from the Bengali entrepreneur Dwarkanath Tagore. Even on its own terms as a debate about the rights of British subjects, freedom of the press became an avenue for rights-claims within a colonial Indian tradition that was commensurate with 'western' liberalism as it emerged in the early nineteenth century.

IV

As a right, press freedom was claimed in the context of the reform era of the 1820s and 1830s. In this sense, it is part of the wider story of liberalism in the context of colonial India, one that was articulated in the language of its British counterpart. As a cause, it resembled and, in many ways, overlapped with the Anglicist/Orientalist debate in Indian education. Ram Mohan Roy and James Silk Buckingham linked press freedom directly to the growth of western learning in India.[69] More precisely, the free press advocates were part of the same intellectual moment as James Mill's *History of British India* (1817), with its cynical assessment of the militarism and protection of 'traditional' practices exemplified by Sir John Malcolm, John Adam, and other acolytes of Governor General Wellesley. A lengthy attack on Adam in the first issue of Buckingham's *Oriental Herald* observed, 'In that country of Toleration . . . where every species of abomination and atrocity in religion is freely permitted, and even tribute received into the coffers of Government, from these most corrupt of all sources—the toleration of a press unfettered by such restraints as the Governor General, in the exercise of his discretion, may think fit to impose, is declared to be fraught with the most extensive mischiefs! Do we address ourselves to Englishmen, and do not their spirits rise in indignation within them at such a declaration?' In contrast, Malcolm saw press freedom as inimical to imperial rule, stating, 'In other countries . . . the use of the press is gradually extended along with the improvements of the government and the intelligence of the people; but we shall have to contend at once with the most refined theories of Europe, and with the prejudices and fanaticism of Asia, both rendered doubly formidable by the imperfect education of those to who every appeal will be addressed. Is it possible that a foreign government, avowedly maintained by the sword, can long keep its ground under such circumstances?'[70] If, Malcolm observed, the leaders of the government of a military despotism like British India 'act under dread of responsibility, or seek popularity, our danger from their measures will be greater than any that could result even from tyranny; the latter can be checked and punished, but that weakness which, in considering its own safety or gratification, forgets the interests of the state evades all remedy'.[71] For Malcolm, the leading ideologue of Company rule in this period, a press that held government to account was therefore unsuitable for Europeans and for Indians living under imperial rule in British India.[72] The story of how press freedom was regulated and why these restrictions were lifted thus draws together two major strands in the history of Company rule in the early nineteenth century. On the one hand, the radical call for press freedom reminds us of the history of liberal claims-making in India itself. On the other, government attempts to monitor and control the press should be understood in the context of the era of rapid imperial consolidation begun by Wellesley in 1798 (the year before censorship was introduced) and crowned by the declaration of British paramountcy in India in 1818 (the year censorship in Bengal was lifted).

The complexities of regulating the right to freedom of the press in British India demand that we revise our understanding of how and why Indians as colonial subjects were excluded from the enjoyment of the rights of metropolitan British subjects. The idea of a negation or simple denial of certain rights to Indian subjects correlates closely with formal legal definitions of 'European' and 'native'. But it also belies the fact that rights were claimed, granted, and withheld through a process which was uneven. The shifting legal pluralism of British India in the eighteenth and early nineteenth centuries demonstrates that the paradigm of blanket denial of universal rights to certain peoples does not explain the partial, piecemeal, and experimental ways in which imperial sovereignty and the colonial subject were articulated through law.[73] As Frederick Cooper has remarked, otherness was never stable and had to be maintained. One can reflect, as Kolsky does, that in India, the practices of the British colonial state tended to fall short of its rhetorical promises of even-handed and impartial justice.[74] How is one to account for this pattern? As the regulation of the press reveals, the Company's reason of state thinking clashed with the jurisdiction of English law in the three presidencies. In this way, the question of who should enjoy these rights and why was as much about the struggle for liberties as it was about imperial domination. At the very least, the free press issue witnessed a crossover or blurring in these two discursive histories. If India was a site of imperial domination, it was also a site for rights-claiming struggles in the history of British imperial subjecthood. Government restrictions on press freedom in this period were not simply an attempt to impose a fixed and stable European set of ideals upon an inchoate and unstable non-European polity. They were an attempt to give fixity to those European norms.

Chapter 3

Citizens and Subjects in the British and French Empires

I

Any examination of empire as a site for the shaping of European political norms must move beyond the study of a single part of a single empire. The choice of the British and French empires as objects for the study of imperial citizenship invites a number of comparisons. Major contrasts are often observed between British and French histories of citizenship. Liberal opposed to republican is a common contrast, supposedly between a British regime defined by the exercise of rights and a French citizenship enacted through active membership of the republic.[1] In the history of empire, particularly in the nineteenth century, a distinction is also made between modes of governing colonial populations. There is a supposedly British model of colonial populations that lacked the capacity to enjoy the rights of the natural-born English subject and should thus be governed in a manner appropriate to local customs. This is seen to be typified in contexts such as early nineteenth-century British India and large parts of Africa and the Middle East in the early twentieth century. In contrast, the archetypal French model was deemed to be 'assimilation'. In this schema, citizenship or full belonging to the polity required certain characteristics or attributes. The enjoyment of citizenship required assimilation to the norms of the French state. Such contrasts can be better discerned in the formal body of government pronouncements and polemical theorizing than in the practice of governing imperial citizenship. It is a central premise of this book that such sharp contrasts tell us little about the practice of governing or being governed as a political subject under empire. To the extent that they tell us much about the experience of British and French citizen and empire, it is the features they have in common as much as the contrasts that are a central concern of this book.

This chapter develops an overall framework for thinking about political belonging under the French and British empires and the emergence of aspects of citizenship in this period. It has three aims. The first is to explore how the practices and forms of British subjecthood and French citizenship in the nineteenth and twentieth centuries have been understood historically. As will be seen, in both Britain and France narratives for understanding citizenship as historically constituted have both been profoundly politicized and subjected to change over time. The limitations of such narratives for rendering a history of imperial citizenship and the effects that they have had on the conception of that history will be discussed. I will then go on to outline the main ways in which the British and French empires in the first half of the nineteenth century were part of a shared history of imperial forms of political belonging and control. A crucial innovation is to introduce both, not as exclusively metropolitan but as traditions formed in and through contact with foreign and often non-European groups. In doing so, the chapter integrates a discussion of these concepts with ideas of association and assimilation, genocide and co-existence as strategies for managing different populations. My aim here is to fill out the argument of the previous chapter. The supposed universalism of modern national citizenship belies the gradations that are a noticeable feature of imperial citizenship. As the examples of the British and French empires in the nineteenth century show, imperial citizenship cannot be comprehended by binary divisions between colonizer and colonized or citizen and foreigner.

II

As we have seen, the history of citizenship is bound up with a dynamic process of reconstituting the past. Any attempt to reconceive citizenship in an imperial rule must open up rather than put aside the historic national vision of citizenship in Britain and France. A useful starting point is to consider some of the dominant ways in which contemporary conceptions of British and French citizenship have understood the past. My emphasis here is on how these renderings of the history of contemporary citizenship have excluded or distanced the role of colonialism in their account.

As we have seen, it is commonplace of contemporary scholarship to view France and Britain as loci for distinct models of citizenship that emerged following the European Enlightenment—the liberal and the civic-republican.[2] In this view, the liberal Anglophone model represents the citizen as an autonomous individual whose freedom to thrive depended on collective guarantees. The civic-republican model constituted the citizen as 'a member of a political community whose ability to participate depended on the integrity of the social order'.[3] In this view, 'citizenship' is a meaningful idea in modern French history. However, in British history it can only be used tentatively and retrospectively. To give an example, throughout the long history of political thought in Britain, citizenship both in language and in substance has nearly always been a theme in a minor key; it has been secondary to and largely overshadowed by more dominant themes such as liberty, property, sovereignty, utility, collectivism versus individualism, and markets versus the state. Moreover, on the relatively rare occasions when 'citizenship' issues have preoccupied British political theorists and public figures, their major concern has not been with the largely taken-for-granted question of who should possess citizenship.[4]

Examining how the idea of British citizenship has been conceived historically provides a starting point for understanding the exclusion of colonial aspects and how they might be incorporated. In a series of lectures delivered in 1949 and later published as *Citizenship and Social Class*, the British sociologist T. H. Marshall described modern citizenship of the nation-state as a series of civil, political, and social rights that had been successively gained.[5] Marshall argued that the distinctions between the three sets of rights drew from the separate historical origins of the national institutions that administered them, namely the courts, parliament, and lastly the state as a provider of welfare. For Marshall, the expansion of each enabled the growth of the others. In the nineteenth century, parliament was to be a forum for the greater protection of civil rights. He noted, 'It was . . . appropriate that nineteenth-century capitalist society should treat political rights as a secondary product of civil rights. It was equally appropriate that the twentieth century should abandon this position and attach political rights directly and independently to citizenship as such'.[6] After this transformation, the welfare state was to ensure the capacity of the electorate to participate in political life. This itself represented the end of a long period where the acceptance of welfare as a right had entailed the giving up of effective citizenship rights:

> The Poor Law treated the claims of the poor, not as an integral part of the rights of the citizen, but as an alternative to them—as claims which could be met only if the claimants ceased to be citizens in any true sense of the word. For paupers forfeited in practice the civil right of personal liberty, by internment in the workhouse, and they forfeited by law any political rights they might possess. This disability of disfranchisement remained in being until 1918. . . . The stigma which clung to poor relief expressed the deep feelings of a people who understood that those who accepted relief must cross the road that separated the community of citizens from the outcast company of the destitute.[7]

Marshall's historical vision of citizenship assumed its formation from separate sites of rights claiming. This was a central part of the character of citizenship as a national institution. Political rights had emerged to protect the civil rights of a capitalist class in the nineteenth century. However, the centrality of political rights in the twentieth century could only be secured by the enjoyment of social rights as part of citizenship rights. As the welfare example shows, Marshall's various phases of the development of national citizenship were marked by the dominance of one particular aspect of citizenship rights, and the groups that it benefited, at the expense of marginalization and disenfranchisement. The same can be said about imperial citizenship yet with broader consequences than those implied by Marshall.

The imperial scale amplifies this multiple-sited institutional aspect of the formation of citizenship understood as rights and belonging. It also brings to the fore questions of minority rights, race, gender, and contested claims of territorial sovereignty that were not part of Marshall's conception of citizenship. For T. H. Marshall, the eighteenth century had witnessed the emergence of a corpus of civil rights, protected in law, that curtailed the power of government over the individual. Increasingly, the ability of Parliament, as representative of the people, to maintain its independence in relation to the Crown was seen as indicative of this, heralding a new primacy for political rights. If we take this one example of Parliament, it soon becomes evident that what Marshall saw as evidence of the formation of a national institution can be described just as convincingly in terms of empire. Moreover, the imperial context presents the ascendency of the civil, the political, and the social as partial, fleeting, and significantly complicated by the shifting multi-jurisdictional contexts of British imperial space in the nineteenth and twentieth centuries.

Even according to Marshall's categories of civil, political, and social rights, the institutions and practices that interested him had colonial dimensions. In terms of the civil, British subjects lived under a range of jurisdictions with sets rights that were often unclear or the subject of negotiation. Many issues remained unresolved. For example, over the 123 years of the Hanoverian succession, it had never been determined whether or not citizens of Hanover were British subjects.[8] Across the British Empire, the sources of law varied considerably from English law administered in Crown colonies, to laws promulgated by colonial assemblies, to subjecthood determined by legal treaty. Hannah Weiss Muller has argued that over the course of the eighteenth century, through conquest many Catholics enjoyed rights as British subjects in colonial possessions that they would not have had under the restrictions on Catholics that prevailed in Britain itself.[9] This can be seen in contexts as varied as Trinidad, Upper Canada, and Malta. As a later chapter will show, the East India Company had the power to deport Europeans, including Britons. This was an instance where Indian subjects of the British Empire had a protection that their British-born counterparts did not. As these examples suggest, colonial contexts provide examples that confound Marshall's model. Both at the colonial level and in Britain itself, many groups faced severe formal restrictions where their civil and political rights were concerned. Jewish emancipation for instance occurred in Canada in 1831, Jamaica in 1832, and Great Britain itself in 1858, over two decades later. Moving to the social, throughout the 1820s and 1830s, there were several efforts to establish colonies of paupers in the British Empire. Yet recipients of poor law relief who emigrated to settlement colonies in Canada, Australia, or New Zealand might find themselves enfranchised, enjoying political rights. Marshall's schema therefore says little about the place of group differentiation and discrimination in the development of citizenship.

Marshall's three strands of civil, political, and social rights take on a different significance depending on whether we see the British Empire as a single imperial polity that incorporated Britain and its various overseas possessions, or whether these possessions are viewed as mere colonies, granted limited devolved authority. Mithi Mukherjee has recently interpreted this as a long running tension between what she calls the colonial and the imperial. The colonial, on the one hand, emphasizes the rights of conquest of a sovereign over territories that are ruled as colonies. Mukherjee roots the colonial mode in the political thought of Thomas Hobbes. As she explains, 'In this colonial or Hobbesian model, the state's need for the consent of the people was indistinguishable from the need for their obedience; the people did not need to express their consent through representational practices such as elections'.[10] She adds, 'Any responsibilities of the government towards the people derived not from its legal accountability to the people, but from the moral sense of the rule or the state'.[11] On the other hand, the imperial mode assumes that all the people who live within the imperial polity are subject to the same laws. Mukherjee sees this epitomized in and largely originating from Edmund Burke's writings on empire. In Burkean discourse, according to Mukherjee, the colonial state in India had 'legitimacy on the basis of how it carried out its legal and moral responsibilities towards the colonized society'. Notwithstanding the need for a more historically nuanced rendering of the intellectual lineages of these two traditions, Mukherjee's schema reminds us that the formation of rights continually brought to the fore a tension between the belonging of the individual to a large imperial polity and the institutional divisions within that polity that generated differential categories of 'citizenship'. This enables us to understand limited and partial expressions of rights by colonial subjects as part of a dynamic tension in the nature of imperial citizenship between unity and difference. Where Marshall's scheme ends quite neatly with the ascendency of the social in mid-twentieth-century Britain, incorporating the experience of colonialism amplifies the tension between the social, the political, and the civil.

Mukherjee's framing of colonial subjecthood also reveals another vital aspect of the British subject in this period: the protection afforded by the British Crown when travelling in foreign lands. Before 1905, British subjects scarcely had more rights than foreigners in British territory.[12] Unlike certain civil rights, such as habeas corpus which applied to anyone whether or not they were a British subject, rights of protection were a distinct manifestation of British power and authority in relation to the individual. One of the chief benefits of being a British subject was protection in foreign lands. As Dummett notes, British subjecthood actually could refer to collection of different nationalities: It was often the case before the nineteenth century that locally naturalized subjects claimed only the rights of protected persons. Crucially, for foreign powers there was no difference between a protected person and a subject—the difference only existed within the empire.[13] In Adam McKeown's view by the end of the nineteenth century, the term imperial subject had proved inadequate to the task of regulating free migration. Citizenship came to replace it as ideas of race and nation gained prominence.[14] While McKeown's focus was the nation-building of the white settler colonies of the British Empire, his observation applies equally well to many other 'western' contexts in the same period, particularly France and the United States. We can, of course, incorporate the longer history of capitulations or exemptions from local jurisdiction that powers such as France and Britain claimed through treaties in the Ottoman and Chinese empires.[15] The rights and protection of the subject abroad seem to be an important precursor of contemporary citizenship that is absent from a largely domestic account of its origin. Plenty of accounts have considered the role of aliens, strangers, refugees, metics, and similar identities as agonistic aspects of the formation of citizen. The projection and protection of that citizen or subject abroad in foreign lands is an equally important but largely neglected aspect.

Marshall's view of citizenship is still used as a point of entry for studies of citizenship across the world, often without an appreciation of its specific British (arguably English) context or of the fact that it presents an historical model of the gradual formation of modern citizenship. His geographically and historically situated vision of citizenship, rendered from the vantage of mid-twentieth-century Britain, is often treated as something like a normative statement about the structure and form of citizenship. Even critiques have done little to replace its threefold scheme of the civil, political, and social.[16] Inadequate as it is in so many ways for understanding citizenship around the world today, Marshall's view of citizenship as a series of convergences of historical patterns has much to commend itself in how we might understand the emergence of British imperial citizenship, even if this is a topic Marshall himself had little to say about. Notwithstanding its shortcomings, Marshall's model reminds us that we are tracing the history of an institution before it was named as such. The historian of what constitutes citizenship has a deeper task than closely contextualizing the emergence and use of the term 'citizen'. To trace the historical formation of various elements that would come to be called citizenship is the task at hand in describing and analyzing imperial citizenship. Of interest is not the contextual specificity of the name but the historical circumstance that created the forms of belonging and the repertoires of action that we associate with contemporary citizenship.

In contrast to the British experience, the term 'citizen' has been a politically freighted concept in much of the literature on France and its empire from the French Revolution onward. Two preliminary observations are useful for understanding how to draw together the national framing of French citizenship and the role of colonial experience. First, frequent evocation of a stable concept of the citizen belies the shifts in its meaning and significance over time. This might, at first glance, seem a rather banal observation. As will be seen, the battle for the historical context and meaning of citizenship in French political and intellectual life has been so prominent that only a limited comparison can be made with nearest equivalents in British history such as the liberties of the freeborn English subject. Secondly, a common aspect of these debates has been a tension between the citizen and the nation. Central to this question is the role of supposed national characteristics in the criteria of who can be a citizen and what constitutes citizenship. Following from this, a recurrent theme has been a question of whether France can incorporate multiple national groups and whether it should recognize national differences in the provision of civil and political rights. As will be seen, this last point invites a strong comparison with Britain in the same period.

Addressing the first question, the concepts of the republic and the citizen—prominent aspects of the French Revolution and of contemporary French thought—have not been constant. Shifting narratives about the past play such a central role in the construction of citizen and republic in modern France. As Adrian Favell and Emile Chabal remind us, the vision of a stable set of republican values at the center of French citizenship is a politicized historical myth that bears little scrutiny as a mode for understanding the nineteenth and twentieth centuries and the changes that occurred during them.[17] The neo-republicanism of the later twentieth century did much to cement this idea. Even counter-narratives such as Gérard Noiriel's *The French Melting Pot*, which attempted to overturn ideas of national cultural homogeneity, mostly covered inflows of European migrants and had nothing to say about colonial subjects. For Noiriel, France and the United States were the two democratic nations that had received the largest numbers of migrants over the course of the nineteenth and twentieth centuries. Yet it was only in the United States that scholars had demonstrated the centrality of migrants to the shaping of modern national identity.[18] Noiriel's preoccupation was to reinstate Jewish populations and European migrants in the history of French politics and society. He saw the restoration of migration to a central place in French history as a political act, challenging historical traditions that identified citizenship with preferred national characteristics.[19] As the historian of Algerian independence, Benjamin Stora has argued that the development of a historiography of migration from former colonies from the 1980s was a form of political activism animated by antagonism to dominant neo-republican historical narratives in French universities and public life.[20] The significance of the colonial in the formation of French citizenship has not been simply undervalued or ignored but deliberately suppressed by a counter-narrative in contemporary French public life.

Moving to the second point, the idea of the nation and who can be a part of it has been a matter of prolonged and intricate debate. In one respect, this is a question of how we are to understand the supposed universalism of French citizenship in the context of what appears to be the assertion of certain cultural practices over others. As Cécile Laborde puts it, 'While citizenship is undoubtedly defined by a tension between inclusion and exclusion, what characterizes the French conception is a paradoxical, almost schizophrenic, commitment to both an abstract universalism and a strong concept of the political community as a clearly bounded geographical and ethical space'.[21] Dominique Colas adds, political citizenship founded on national criteria has been the limit of national citizenship. For Noiriel, this assumption of a kind of national homogeneity, of a 'rooted' community necessary for access to citizenship, has been a dominant feature of French historiography from the mid-nineteenth century onward.[22] However, much recent historical writing has nuanced this interpretation. For example, Eugene Weber's argument that the Third Republic saw a concerted program of centralization that steadily and confidently turned peasants into Frenchmen has been refuted.[23] In the same vein, Gary Wilder, Frederick Cooper, and others have argued for a more central place for alternative renderings of citizenship as rights claiming. As Cooper has observed about the distinction between French citizens and French colonial subjects, it was 'as insidious as it is often portrayed but not so fixed an attribute'.[24] In other words, there were differences between citizens and subjects that often had real consequences, but definitions and applications were often fluid and inconsistent. Moreover, when movements in different contexts took on the term citizenship it acquired new meaning. The point is that Noiriel, Balibar, and others were right to identify a dominant discourse of national homogeneity underpinning claims about who could be a

French citizen. However, the effect of highlighting such features of political discourse has been to overemphasize their significance.

In some ways the process of historicizing French citizenship invites us not only to search for the origins of this paradox but also to see in the present an oversimplification of the evidence of complex processes in the past. In other words, this homogenized historical image shaped not only celebrations but also radical critique of French citizenship. This can be seen, for example, by returning to Étienne Balibar's rendering of the supposed revolutionary origins of modern European citizenship: 'The modern democratic nation (resulting from the great 'bourgeois revolutions', which we should not forget also means, following the etymology, revolutions in citizenship), whose principles gave rise to 'declarations of the rights of man and the citizen' or their equivalent, fundamentally excludes by denaturing those reputed to be incapable of autonomous judgment, that is, by inventing anthropological alterity, whose major variables are sex, race, morality, health, and physical or mental age'.[25] If this is a picture that we recognize, do we agree that it has been integral to modern citizenship since its origins? As we have seen, a drawback of such historicized visions of contemporary citizenship is that it underplays the history of radical reconstitution and resistance which is a part of citizenship. This approach also takes this history to be a set of essentially national narratives, underplaying the full significance of the legacy of colonial polities in shaping the modern institution of citizenship.

The study of British and French imperial citizenship requires the displacement of a closed conception of national citizenship and a disruption of dominant narratives that have been used to articulate it. In both cases, the sense of inevitability and uniformity must be challenged. As we have seen, recent scholarship on national as well as colonial contexts makes this possible. At the same time, the rhetorical force of the dominant narratives should also be an object of study. In part, this is because these narratives have influenced ideas about citizenship and in part because it enables a better understanding of how and why they affect our understanding of the formation of contemporary citizenship.

III

Differences in rhetorical framing belie a common experience of subjecthood in British and French colonial contexts. This shared experience offers some insights into links between an apparent shared institution of citizenship among western nations and a common past of imperial aggrandizement. If this book is an attempt to question entrenched ideas of contrast and difference between the two exemplars, it also recognizes the impact of these interpretations. The following section therefore sketches out some of these constructions and their relative significance in rendering a common history of imperial citizenship in the British and French empires in the early nineteenth century.

The first observation to make is that throughout most of the nineteenth century, France and Britain shared a common experience as liberal imperial powers. As we have seen, there is a perception that France developed a civic republican model of the citizen as part of a community comprised in the nation and Britain was the crucible of an individual-centered, rights-based form of citizenship. Both owe much to a politicized contemporary narrative about the past and both belie significant common elements in their histories. Certainly, in the 1830s and 1840s, France and Britain were both understood to be the crucible of the social and economic progress that liberalism was seen to promise.[26] Both France and Britain experienced a long period of change as imperial polities from the mid-eighteenth century, through the French and American revolutions, to the liberal empires of the mid-nineteenth century. Of course, the French and British colonial empires were only part of this story. As Josep Fradera has argued, the growing power of the fiscal-military state created a friction with large and growing populations of rights-claiming subjects in the metropoles and peripheries of Atlantic facing colonial powers.[27] In the decades following the French Revolutionary and Napoleonic Wars, Britain and France bore a close resemblance to each other. In the 1820s, both had limited monarchical governments led by aristocratic ministries with rural power bases.[28] In the following years, political pressure from growing and increasingly organized middle-class and working-class urban populations created an impetus for political reform that came to a head in both Britain and France in the early 1830s. The July Revolution in France, coinciding as it did with unrest in Britain over the reform bill confirmed a sense of a shared political journey.

Contemporary commentators drew the comparisons, even as they noted their limitations. As John Stuart Mill, a major contributor to this discourse, observed in 1846, 'The two strongest tendencies of the world in these times are towards Democracy and Revolution. . . . In this twofold career, France is the furthest advanced of the European nations'.[29] Yet, as Mill noted, 'The fact is not necessarily of the highly complimentary character with which [French] writers generally choose to invest it. . . . To be foremost in the road which all are travelling, is not of necessity the most honourable position'.[30] Bemoaning the lack of protection given to free speech or due process in France, Walter Bagehot wrote, 'There does not seem to be now in France, any more than at any previous period, the slightest conception of, or care for what we in England call personal liberty—the liberty of the subject'.[31] A leitmotif of British commentary on France was this supposed lack of civil rights and the proud sense of personal liberty that protected them. Mill, Bagehot, and other writers frequently drew a distinction between British civilization characterized by practical achievement and material prosperity and the French marked by a more abstract intellectual brilliance and increasing centralization.[32] This was a commonplace that owed something to Burke's *Reflections on the Revolution in France* (1790) and would gain support as the century drew on. The revolution of 1848, Louis Napoleon's coup d'état of 1851, and his self-proclamation as emperor would all ultimately dissipate this sense of affinity between liberal nations.

During the 1830s and 1840s, a broad political alignment between Britain and France was accompanied by cooperation on a number of key foreign and colonial policy matters. The return of Napoleon's body to France by the British government in 1840 and a visit by Prince Louis Philippe to Britain in 1844 were visible signs of closeness.[33] More substantively, the period was characterized by sustained transnational cooperation between Britain and France as they conquered and exploited extra-European possessions—for instance, between European settlers in the Caribbean islands.[34] The period saw the rise of philanthropic interest in international causes such as the abolition of slavery, the welfare of indigenous peoples, and the protection of Jewish populations in the Mediterranean.[35] In all these matters, frequent alignment of interests between the British and French governments was matched by a common sphere of public debate. Crucially, the social groups and networks that campaigned for such causes in each country thought able to address themselves to similar causes and similar audiences in the other country. This can be seen for instance with the cause of emancipation in France.[36] It can also be seen in the field of indigenous rights. The English lawyer Saxe Bannister's *Appel en Faveur d'Alger, et de l'Afrique du Nord, par un Anglais* (1833) is one example of this. The Anglo-French free-trade agreement of 1861 was a significant moment enshrining *inter alia* freedom of movement between the two nations. For instance, the presence of 20,000 British metallurgical workers in northern France was a key aspect of French industrialization during the 1840s.[37] Britain and France saw themselves as near equivalents in a common enterprise of civilizational improvement.

However, British and French colonial expansion and control entailed forms and levels of violence that strained the developed of peaceful, stable polities in Britain and France themselves. From the late eighteenth century onward, politicians and commentators asked if liberty at home would be compromised by the violent conquest and control of colonial possessions abroad.[38] At the same time, metropolitan Britain and France themselves were sites of significant violent unrest, for example in 1830 and 1848. In the milieu of British and French liberals, the former tended to see the latter as barbaric in their justification of colonial violence, notably Tocqueville's defense of razzia (burning of villages and farmlands). Tocqueville said Algeria needed a new kind of warfare and defended razzias, not for extermination but for military victory.[39] At the same time, Tocqueville denounced the British for their hypocrisy. As he said of them, 'What I cannot get over is their perpetual attempts to prove that they act in the interest of a principal, or for the good of the natives, or even for the advantages of the sovereigns they subjugate . . . these are the procedures with which they almost always surround violence'. Something of the cant Tocqueville deplored in the British can be found in the following *Edinburgh Review* article of 1846:

> If Clive had landed in India with 70,000 men, and proceeded at the head of that army to attack every race, every religion, and every prince of the Mogul Empire, he might have swept over the land at the head of such an irresistible force; but he would not have ensured the pacific administration of the British Empire in India. That Empire is the splendid result, not of mere conquest, but of conquest guided, controlled, and moderated by policy and civil government; and in spite of the manifest differences between the population of India and of Barbary, policy and civil government, founded on the great principles of human nature and civilized society, are the only basis of lasting dominion.[40]

Throughout the decades of the mid-nineteenth century, British rule in India provided British and French observers alike with a model and testing ground for colonial conquest and government. Commentators at the time and many subsequent historians have contrasted a French empire characterized by the aim of assimilating colonial populations to a British empire marked by the maintenance of local customs. The cautious approach to British India was typified by the romantic conservatism of administrators such Sir John Malcolm and Sir Thomas Munro and later adapted by Sir Henry Maine and others.[41] During the 1850s and 1860s, the French ruler Napoleon III took British India as his model when he attempted to build Algeria as an Arab Kingdom under French rule. For all those who saw British India as a successful model of cautious population management, there were many in both the British and French empires that saw this as a negligent form of imperial rule. This is because it failed to share the benefits of European civilization with colonial populations.

In other words, assimilation was part of the liberal case for reform during this period. This can be seen in aspects of British and French rule during the 1830s and 1840s. In the British Empire, utilitarian and other groups saw the colonial possessions and British India in particular as opportunities to enact improving schemes in a context unshackled by the conventions and structures of European polities.[42] As Belmessous has noted, assimilation aimed not so much at turning colonial subjects into Europeans but seizing the opportunity of colonial rule to make better Europeans.[43] This can be seen in the reforming ambitions of the Bentinck government of British India in the 1820s—for instance, in his efforts to increase peasant proprietorship at the expense of large landholders. Equally, Algeria would become, among other things, an ideal locus for socially experimental groups of settlers.[44] In practice assimilation and its pluralistic alternatives were features of colonial rule that can be found in both the British and the French contexts.

In both empires, slavery and emancipation raised questions about the rights of the individual under empire. The question of capacity to enact freedom is a central issue in traditional, western-focused histories of citizenship. Throughout the period, the abolition of slavery, or the granting of freedom to individual slaves, created or exposed new barriers to the equal enjoyment of rights and fulfillment of obligations under the imperial polity. The years between the abolition of slavery in the British Empire in 1833 and in the French colonies in 1848 were a mutually constitutive moment. For both, slavery presented a clear contradiction to metropolitan ideas of citizenship and subjecthood. France had abolished slavery in the Revolution, reinstated it under Napoleon, and would not abolish it again until 1848. Britain abolished the slave trade in 1807 and slavery in 1833. As Alexis de Tocqueville said to the National Assembly in 1846: 'The English are doing nothing at the moment but applying our principles in their colonies. . . . Will France, the democratic country *par excellence*, remain the sole European nation to patronize slavery?'[45] Even in abolition, both empires were dominated by the question of how to govern and provide for the prosperity of populations that had suffered historic injustice. Laurent Dubois has suggested French 'universalism' was in fact in many ways produced through the actions of slaves in the Caribbean. The struggles around slave emancipation and political equality in the Caribbean that developed during the French Revolution produced, in Dubois's view, a Republican tradition of antiracist egalitarianism, yet also '"Republican racism" through which new practices of exclusion were articulated'.[46] The Haitian revolution was both a symbol of terrifying and unruly black rebellion for authorities in Britain and France and an iteration of the citizenly ideals of the French Revolution capable of providing inspiration to colonized peoples throughout the nineteenth century.[47] This is a useful way of understanding the legacy not just of the Haitian Revolution but of other attempts to instigate radical political agendas in former slave colonies. The politics of emancipation reveals an array of rights-claiming actions that strained the limitations of imperial citizenship.

During the nineteenth century, both France and Britain promoted the mass migration of populations to found settler colonies. Throughout the nineteenth century, they both vacillated in their view of what groups in society should be settlers. Britain had experimented with both convict transportation and so-called pauper colonies, as a means of peopling new territories while alleviating social problems at home. In the early decades of French colonization of Algeria, similar methods were adopted. The French government's vision of great swathes of small peasant land holdings failed because they were too reliant on settler migration as a way of reducing the French urban population.[48] As one contemporary American observer of French colonization noted, 'There is but one opinion, that the colonists sent out are not of the right kind'.[49] In British North America and Australia during the 1820s and 1830s and in French Algeria in the 1830s and 1840s, there was a concern that settlers all too often lacked the ethno-linguistic identity or the social class to be effective conduits of European civilization. At the same time, settlers themselves attempted to enact metropolitan rights in the context of the presence of large populations without such rights. These debates turned on the question of why Europeans must be governed in accordance with a set of rights that often exceeded those available in the metropole, for example in terms of the franchise. The settler colonies provide an important, and still under-researched, venue for the discussions of autonomy, gender, class, national identity, and race that were such integral aspects of the metropolitan history of democratization and citizenship in British and French thought.

In both British and French empires, tensions existed between the civic and political life of the metropole and the periphery, that is, their colonial possessions. As Josep Fradera has argued, from the 1780s onward, the Atlantic imperial monarchic empires gave way to ruptures between colonial populations and central governments. British commentators felt that a major feature of French thought entirely absent from Britain was Bonapartism, the belief in the redeeming powers of a strong, popular leader. In the French national context, British writers saw this as inconsistent with liberal protection of the rights of the individual.[50] This also has implications for the understandings of Algeria as an extension of the French state. If Algeria was ruled through the presence of a vast army, governing by martial law, the separation of the empire from the metropole was seen as essential to those liberties that were seen to define Great Britain as the preeminent liberal nation.

IV

In both contemporary Britain and France, a dominant historical account of the citizen sees its origin in the metropolitan nation rather than empire. In Britain, this vision of the origins of modern citizenship is associated with T. H. Marshall. In France, as I have argued, the parameters of the debate have been shaped by a range of neo-republican writers and politicians. These narratives, for all their differences, both invite a view of migration from former colonies after World War II as something without precedent that strained early notions of national citizenship. A rich counter-narrative is possible that incorporates the ways in which issues of belonging, group-rights, racism, authoritarianism, and other aspects of the history of citizenship. These aspects of citizenship are best understood in a broadly imperial context over a much longer historical period than the era of decolonization and the postwar welfare state. This counter-narrative necessitates an investigation into the common origins of both modern citizenship and modern empires in the early decades of the nineteenth century.

The history of Britain and France in the first half of the nineteenth century does not provide parallel origin stories for liberal and republican citizenship. Rather, both shared a common experience of piecemeal political and civil reform at home combined with imperial expansion characterized both by authoritarianism and social experimentation. This led to a growth of plural jurisdictions in response to governing both new colonial populations and groups of European settlers. This generated a contrast between metropole defined by recognition of rights and a relatively homogenous population and different peripheries marked by the management of a mix of local customs and in most cases military government, the so-called *regime de sabre*. Rather than being a paradox, as a large body of scholarly writing on liberalism and empire has shown, the liberal core and the illiberal periphery co-constituted. In both cases, this uneasy mix of rights regimes was delivered through a blend of assimilation and association. It generated a contemporary debate—on British India as a model of imperial rule and on the abolition of slavery—which combined British and French public spheres. Using the example of the French invasion of Algeria, the next chapter will explore how this common public sphere addressed issues of invasion, conquest, and colonization.

Chapter 4

Britain and the French Invasion of Algeria, 1830–1870

I

If British traditions of the political subject were shaped by empire and by struggles with neighboring France, how were they influenced by the French empire? In attempting to identify, trace, and expose the subjectivities, practices, and discourses that comprised European imperialism culturally and politically, much of what we are looking for remains hidden under the supposed dividing lines between different imperial enterprises. This chapter uses British discourse on the French invasion of Algeria from 1830 to 1870 to analyze how imperial subjecthood was constituted across the multiple sites where empire was experienced. The analysis of British discourse on French Algeria provides a brief example of the ways in which the European political subject was constituted not simply in opposition to non-European colonial populations but also in the interplay of different European experiences of imperial domination. It does so by studying how British imperial commentators understood 'invasion' as a model of imperial expansion and by examining contemporary comparisons between French Algeria and British India as militarized colonial societies.

Analytically, it is clear that the borders of metropolitan empires do not mark the boundaries of those strategies of knowledge creation that generated practices and discourses associated with imperial domination such as orientalism, biological racism, genocide, or forms of legal pluralism.[1] Contemporary British understandings of empire are studied here in the crosscurrent between two intellectually and culturally distinct imperial enterprises. Such an intellectual history allows us to understand precisely how British ideas of the subject in the context of empire were shaped by both French and non-Western imperial 'others'. Divergent and opposing intellectual histories of French and British concepts of the imperial have been encouraged by a tendency to see metropolitan cultural production as distinct to those metropoles and their colonies. By extension, colonial enterprise has often been seen to be conceptually contained within national politics and diplomatic rivalry.[2] France and the French did provide an 'other' for the formation of British nation identity and the articulation of British political discourses. In an imperial context, one can see this in the blame for rebellion assigned to the political and social atavism of French settlers in Canada in the Durham Report of 1839.[3] At the same time, a pronounced feature of this period was a sense of common enterprise among fellow liberal constitutional monarchies in the Europe of the Congress of Vienna system, dominated by autocratic powers.[4]

My argument here builds on a body of research that has sought to identify the limits and exceptions to a general pattern of anti-French sentiment forming a sense of political belonging among Britons.[5] The historiography of both imperialism and orientalism continues to occlude discourses formed across these national metropolitan boundaries.[6] The 'new imperial history' has successfully blurred the separation of British metropolitan and imperial histories.[7] Yet most studies in this vein work within the spatial limits of the British Empire, or at least the 'Anglo-sphere'. Such exceptionalism belies the fact that many of the people, places, and ideas that constituted British imperial sites cut across the limits of Britain's empire and through other European imperial and non-imperial spaces. This has been brought out very convincingly in the growing body of work on what has been called the colonial civic order.[8] The approach of Elizabeth Thompson and others enables us to identify both what was common, what was distinct, and what was in conflict at the points where European imperial orders were constituted alongside each other.

To call British and French cooperation and mutual exchange of ideas in Algeria simply a European enterprise is to disregard the ways in which this 'European-ness' was itself fractured along national cultural lines and constituted through such ventures. An obvious example discussed here is the effect of Protestantism on the articulation of a language of progress used in an anglophone context to describe the imperial endeavors of a Catholic country.⁹ Supposedly transnational European discourses, such as humanitarianism (a common feature of the material discussed), were nevertheless mediated and articulated through distinct metropolitan cultural and political norms. Separate 'national' projects and norms combined, overlapped, and interlinked to create a sense of what European civilization meant but this was articulated through distinct political languages.

This chapter uses British discourses on the French conquest of Algeria from invasion in 1830 to the collapse of the Second Empire in 1870. The consolidation of French power in Algeria occurred in the context of an unusual moment of affinity where both Britain and France identified themselves as liberal, constitutional monarchies and each was able to tolerate the presence of the other in their imperial spheres. The Great Reform Act of 1832 was a highpoint in the creation of British political identity and the following two decades heralded a new phase of imperial consolidation.[10] The July Monarchy of 1830 in France and the invasion of Algeria marked a comparable phase for France. Domestically, both were widely understood to be reforming liberal constitutional monarchies; a parallel image slowly eroded by events in France, culminating in the declaration of the Third Republic in 1870.[11]

My argument about the ways in which the French invasion of Algeria reconfigured British perceptions of empire contributes to critiques of the supposed contrast between imperial practices of 'association' and 'assimilation', between a liberal British metropole that imposed 'traditional' political structures on indigenous colonial populations and a republican French metropole that attempted to reproduce its own political subjectivities and concurrent rights and obligations among its colonial peoples.[12] Even as a heavily qualified generalization, this pattern is more appropriate to the period after 1870. Indeed, this apparent contrast has been extenuated by the Third Republic's break with the imperial politics of Napoleon III and its reassertion of the republican vision of citizenship as participation, combined with the reemergence of indirect rule and association in British imperial thought after the Indian Uprising (1857), the Morant Bay rebellion (1865), and the Maori wars (1860s).[13] In British imperial thought, particularly in the context of India, confidence in reform and assimilation were features of the period between 1830 and 1857 that blunted any contrast between the French and British conceptions of the imperial subject.[14]

This chapter can only indicate the broad trends evident from a representative sample of the material available regarding a complex but under-researched analytical field in the history of European discourses on non-European peoples, colonial knowledge, and imperial state-building. My main sources are those writings which specifically compared the British and French enterprises. These include a large sample of contemporary travel accounts, histories, military and diplomatic memoirs, and contemporary journalism together with diplomatic records for the ambassador to France and the Consul of Algiers. Unlike the Levant, a site of pilgrimage, or the United States, Algeria was not extensively written about by any major British commentator or author in this period.[15] As will be seen, aspects of the French conquest, such as the 'razzia' (tactical burning of civilian farmlands and stores) or the resistance of Abd al-Qādir received considerable mention at certain flashpoints such as the latter's defeat in 1847. In this sense, many of the topics match those found in contemporary French accounts of Algeria.[16] The passing comments and occasional asides of a few significant writers, such as Friedrich Engels and John Stuart Mill, are briefly discussed only because they are significant as the astute observations of major commentators intellectually capable of integrating their observations on French Algeria into a British schema of multiple colonies on a global scale. More generally, I demonstrate that the history of liberal thought and its relationship to the patterns of empire can only be imperfectly studied through the unrepresentative brilliance, sophistication, and limited specialist interest of a few canonical theorists.[17]

The shift away from canonical political thought toward genres such as travel, memoir, history, and journalism enables a better analysis of activities or identities that were deemed to constitute political participation in the colonial polity.[18] It foregrounds different milieus of writers, with a greater proportion of soldiers, women, religious nonconformists, and missionaries.[19] Missionaries such as Ellen Rogers put their efforts into the conversion not of native Muslim populations but of the French, Spanish, and Jewish. Rogers emphasized Protestantism as the distinguishing marker of the west as the apex of civilization, rather than the racial, cultural, or political affinities between France and Britain as imperial powers. In a representative passage, Rogers noted, 'The readiness with which the French and Spaniards, Germans and Maltese, receive such tidings of salvation as we can offer, makes one often feel that it was worth coming to Algiers for their sakes, if God gives such an opportunity as this'.[20] Rogers provides an example of what Clare Midgley has called 'female social imperialism' but in a context where other Europeans join non-Europeans as objects of curiosity and moral concern.[21] Military accounts from the French, Arab, and Berber camps enable a comparison with British occupation colonies, most notably British India.[22] As will be discussed in more detail later, the military gaze emphasized certain aspects of occupation. A significant feature was the assumption that imperium without dominion—mere conquest by a foreign power—created an obligation to rule according to local customs, which was at odds with French practice on the ground.[23] Missionary authors together with the health tourists that became more common in the 1860s naturally had an interest in the urban ports such as Algiers as crucibles of cosmopolitanism mingling of Eastern and European domestic life.[24] The analysis of the discourse formed by such writers enables an understanding of how in practical terms the rights-bearing liberal political subject was being forged.

The invasion turned Algeria into a French imperial space. As a result, it redefined those British subjects who resided there and wrote about it. The following section analyses how conquest, military occupation, and colonial violence were understood in British discourse. British attitudes to the legality, propriety, and prudence of the French government of Algeria changed as the regime itself expanded territorially at the expense of indigenous power bases and the European population increased. The British understanding of constituent peoples of French Algeria will then be discussed with an emphasis on how they were understood to integrate into the colonial polity. The concluding section draws these strands together. In doing so, it outlines the implications of this argument for the broader study of the link between colonialism and the non-European subject in British and French imperial thought and experience. The French invasion of Algeria not only provided an object of comparison for the British Empire but also more sharply defined it through the reconstitution of European imperial space and the movements of people through it in the Mediterranean.

II

This tension between Algeria as a non-European society and as a site of invasion by a foreign European power is at the crux of British discourse on the invasion of Algeria. British discourse was preoccupied with the obligations that France as an imperial power had to the non-European and European populations it ruled over. The ways in which invasion and the imposition of imperial rule were understood by British observers will now be examined. At this time France was not simply a fellow European power but, almost uniquely, considered to be closely comparable to Britain in the degree of wealth, prosperity, refinement, and political liberty its metropolitan citizens enjoyed. Having considered what implications this has for British perceptions, this section will analyze how the invasion itself was understood. In attempting to evaluate what the French were doing and how they should act as an imperial power, Britons used examples from their own imperial experience. At the same time, many saw French Algeria as a new chapter in the history not only of European contact with the wider world but of European civilization itself. These contours of British discourse on French Algeria are examined here. Three assumptions about French imperial rule—its reckless pursuit of political progress, the neglect of civil liberties, and the lack of material sophistication—were common elements of the British critique of French Algeria.

The prolonged presence of French forces after the invasion of June 1830 provoked a debate in Britain and France about the legality and desirability of extra-European empire in Britain and France. A significant anti-imperial movement in the French National Assembly voiced concern about the propriety and prudence of a continued presence.[25] Following the July revolution in France and the fall of the Duke of Wellington's government in Britain, the British government did what it could to avoid a clear pronouncement. At the conclusion of a series of instructions sent by the Colonial Secretary to the Consul in 1831, the following advice was given:

> You will observe that these instructions are written on the assumption that the Sovereignty of France over Algiers is entirely recognized and that the Algerian territory is to be regarded as permanently annexed to that Country. I need scarcely remark that upon a subject of so much importance and delicacy it is not the intention of Lord Goderich [the Colonial Secretary] to express or even to intimate a position. The assumptions are hypothetical only and for the sake of considering immediate practical questions which you have brought under consideration.[26]

The ambiguity of metropolitan interpretations of international law was not quickly resolved. In 1833, the Tory *Quarterly Review* complained that the newly installed Whig government 'have acquiesced in [France's] occupation of Algiers, and her colonization of an unlimited tract of the African coast of the Mediterranean'.[27] The article called upon the government to press the French to withdraw.[28] As late as 1834, the Consul was still advised by his superiors in London 'to use the utmost caution and reserve with respect to any observation on the French occupancy of Algiers'.[29] If asked for an opinion, the Consul was to state that 'not having received any instructions from this Department and being consequently ignorant of the feeling of His Majesty's Government you do not consider that it falls within your province to enter into any discussion thereon'.[30] The British were in part responding to ambiguity in France itself, but uncertainty about the legal foundations or long-term purpose of the French invasion set the tone for subsequent discussion.

Uncertain as they were about their official position on the French invasion of Algeria, British officials also questioned its prudence. The British Consul in Algiers expressed considerable doubt about French actions and their likely success in a letter to the British Ambassador to France, Earl Granville. The Consul was speculating about the conclusion of a recent French Commission of Enquiry that had been sent to report on the conquest. He noted, 'I believe that their opinions differ as to the course to be pursued but I imagine that their report must be nearly as follow'. He continued:

> That they find the climate, soil, & appearance of this country admirable but that the State of its Govt & progresses in Colonization is exorable; That the natives are obstinately hostile to the French on all points; That nothing but conciliating or exterminating them can make the colony prosper; That the first of these modes is almost impossible; That setting aside the inhumanity of the latter mode an annual expense of 60 or 80 millions will be required for some years, besides an immense armed force; That therefore it will remain for Government to judge whether the expenditure is to be increased. Whether it is to be retained as a mere military position or whether it will, by evacuating it, in the face of great difficulties as to the mode, brave the Amour Propre of the nation [France].[31]

As this chillingly stark summary makes plain, the position of the French was seen to be precarious whatever path they followed. The final sentence shows that the Consul recognized this was both a contentious domestic issue within France and a colonial question.[32]

As a colonial question, it had a moral character that transcended national interests in the view of many British observers. A number of commentators were dismayed at the rapidity and extent of French efforts to replace local elites and bureaucracy. In part, certainly up to 1870, it was felt that conquest gave the French imperium but not dominion; they had the right to rule, but an obligation to observe local norms.[33] The point was made by the humanitarian Saxe Bannister. In his *Appel en faveur d'Algerie*, printed in Paris and addressed to the French, Bannister implored them to respect their initial declaration of May 1830 that they would preserve local customs. 'It is', he declared, 'the duty of honest men to re-establish the rights of the natives'.[34] Significantly, Bannister was evoking the international law of war as it pertained to conquest within Europe as well as in contact with non-European powers.[35] At the same time, it is clear that the norms of British imperial conquest were contradicted through such actions. The clergyman and author Joseph Blakesley, travelling in the 1850s, commented, 'No doubt the French, by acts of unflinching severity, have effectually cowed the native population for at least a generation; but they have as yet done but little to reconcile them to the yoke, and less to inspire a love for European civilisation such as they understand it'.[36] Elsewhere, reflecting disapprovingly on a statue of Napoleon erected in Algiers and inscribed 'He had dreamed this conquest',[37] Blakesley observed, 'Such is considered the most appropriate monument to set up to a man whose favourite saying was, "I shall go down to posterity with the Code in my hand" in a country where the conciliation of the native population is a necessary condition of converting source of enormous expense into one of even moderate profit'.[38] Like Bannister, Blakesley was not challenging the French right of conquest. Rather he was affirming it and the obligations it entailed of ruling in conformity with the practices of the people.

In France as in Britain, many were prepared to argue that the violent suppression of native powers and the replacement of native institutions were the obligations of a civilized power, particularly as the French attempted to expand militarily in the 1840s. In a now infamous article for the Chartist *Northern Star*, following the surrender of Abd al-Qādir in 1847, Friedrich Engels wrote, 'The struggle of the Bedouins was a hopeless one, and though the manner in which brutal soldiers, like [Governor General] Bugeaud, have carried on the war is highly blamable, the conquest of Algeria is an important and fortunate fact for the progress of civilization'.[39] There is a well-established literature that attempts to diminish the importance or relevance of such observations in the *oeuvre* of Marx and Engels.[40] Yet it is worth noting that such views were entirely consistent with a strand of contemporary radical thought that was common in debates about indirect rule in British India.[41] In a similar vein, the Boston lawyer George Ditson observed, 'Many villages were burned, thousands of valuable trees and growing crops swept away, and tons of olive oil poured out like water upon the ground. . . . It will be many years before the country can recover from this terrible blow; but, perhaps it is enough that the tri-color waves from the loftiest peaks of the Djujura'.[42] What is striking here is the acceptance of the necessity of violence not only for order but for prosperity.

A central issue was the ability of a military government not simply to bring order but to protect indigenous rights and practices: to provide not dominion but imperium. Up to a third of all French troops were stationed in Algeria during this period, and with a brief interlude following the fall of the French monarchy in 1848, Algeria was ruled under martial law.[43] As Ellen Rogers observed, 'The first thing which strikes one is, that there is here simply a grand military establishment. Almost every other Frenchman one meets is in uniform. The officers have beautiful horses provided for them and in every respect take precedence of their civilian countrymen'.[44] One military traveller writing after the Indian Uprising drew parallels: 'The French recognized the soundness of our Indian policy in employing the native soldier as a means of holding in safety the conquered land; but at the same time they foresaw that the day might come when disaffection, or mutiny, might creep into the ranks of a regiment purely native'.[45] Some commentators such as Rogers saw military rule as an impediment to lasting and prosperous imperial rule. As Henry Reeve wrote in the *Edinburgh Review*, 'The French . . . have relied on military power to effect what is not to be accomplished by force, but by the cautious interference, control, and influence of civil government'.[46] Yet many viewed military rule as preferable to civilian government. As Blakesley observed, 'One of the greatest obstacles, in fact, which the Government have to surmount in reconciling the native population of North Africa to their newly imposed yoke, arises from their treatment generally by the bourgeoisie, who hate them as the Calcutta shopkeepers do the Hindoos, the more for the fear which underlies their dislike'. He went on to note that 'By the military the common Arab is rarely ill-treated. . . . The high offices of administration are generally filled by persons who feel the responsibility of their position, and act as statesmen, if not as Christians, in their relations to the subject class'.[47] Again, the parallels with Indian debates are stark: indirect rule, authoritarian government, and restrictions on the European population were key elements of the militarism of British India.[48]

One aspect of the British analysis of the military regime in Algeria was its close connection to the metropole. In the British Empire at this time, there was a general assumption that the political and civil rights of the metropolitan subject should not be compromised by the various authoritarian regimes of the empire and that such rights would, when possible, be assured for white settlers too.[49] For British political commentators, a major feature of French thought, entirely absent from Britain, was Bonapartism, the belief in the redeeming powers of a strong, popular leader.[50] In the French national context, British writers saw this as inconsistent with the liberal protection of the rights of the individual. This also has implications for understandings of Algeria as an extension of the French state. It can be seen in Blakesley's unease about the many statues of Napoleon. As he noted, writing after Napoleon III's coup d'état, 'this monument was not set up by the present dynasty, but by its predecessor, under the influence of a desire to make political capital out of old military associations which were imagined to be no longer dangerous'.[51] The military traveller Walmsley took a special interest in the abject condition of the political prisoners sent to Algeria after the coup: 'These people, of every age, class, and position, whose crime was attachment to the Republic, and whose absence from France was necessary to the establishment of the Imperial power, were at once seized, embarked on board ship, conveyed to Algiers'.[52] After recounting their hardships, Warmsley observed, 'Perhaps this was all necessary to the Empire, for with such an excitable nation as the French, the same land could not hold in peace these men and an Imperial Government'.[53] In contrast, France and French Algeria after the coup d'état were part of the same authoritarian regime: empire undermined rather than affirmed the freedom of the citizens of the metropole.

III

The question of how the French empire should be governed was, for the observers discussed here, entirely connected with the issue of how a religiously and ethno-linguistically heterodox population of Europeans and non-Europeans should be managed to produce order and prosperity. As this section discusses, colonists, Jews, Kabyles, and Arabs were all described in terms of how such populations integrated into the colonial polity.

Increasingly, the military saw themselves as protecting indigenous populations from the colonists and British accounts generally reflect misgivings about the settlers as components of an ordered and prosperous polity.[54] One commentator in the *United Service Magazine* remarked, 'With the experience that we have of the hardships and perils that the needy classes of our population will voluntarily undergo for the sake of improving their fortunes, it was only natural to suppose that the same classes in France would joyfully rush across a narrow inland sea'.[55] He concluded, 'Algeria . . . will never, under the French rule, become a great and powerful colony, even admitting that the Government does at last exert itself to the utmost, in order to render it so; for the French not only do not understand the system of colonial legislation, but the people themselves are prepossessed against emigration'.[56] Observers recognized that France, without the population surpluses of contemporary Britain, would be less selective about who it sent out. Frequent comments about the squalid conditions of Spanish and Maltese settlers reinforce this reflection. As Ditson remarked, 'I doubt not that the native often asks himself in what consists the boasted civilization of these foreigners'.[57] 'There is', he remarked of French debates on the topic, 'but one opinion, that the colonists sent out are not of the right kind. Those who come on their own are very few'.[58] Drawing an implicit contrast with the British administration of India, Henry Reeve remarked, 'The effect of the French conquest on the native population of the towns, has been in the highest degree detrimental to its morality and well-being. The . . . endowments for the various purposes of education, charity, and religion, have been confiscated or misappropriated; and the influx of European emigrants will, erelong, reduce the natives to the condition of helots in their own cities'.[59] As in the British settler colonies, metropolitan government increasingly asserted that it had a humanitarian duty to constrain the colonists which was at odds with the colonists' rights as Europeans. For British and French administrators and metropolitan observers, the colonists failed to demonstrate full capacity as a responsible rights-bearing European. Becoming proper colonist—both law abiding and law giving—was a difficult task that required discipline in the form of government regulation.[60] This made the colony a site in which empire set the boundaries of the citizenship rights of 'Europeans'.[61]

Almost every account of the region, including the consular records, recognized the Jews as economic intermediaries who benefitted from the protection of a European imperial power. As Ellen Rogers observed, the Jews of Algiers were 'most necessary to a people who only lived upon piracy, and required an intermediate order between their own, and that of the lawful traders of other nations. Under the French Government, they are of course admitted to equal privileges with the rest of their fellow-subjects'.[62] Warmsley too noted, 'Now under French rule, they enjoy every privilege permitted to any colonist, and a great part of the commerce of the country passes through their hands'.[63] Abigail Green argues that British discourse in this period used the language of 'civilization' and 'humanity' on behalf of the Jews with greater consistency than that of France, where Jewish rights were part of a wider conflict between Catholics and anticlericals.[64] As Albert Memmi noted of a later period, the protection of the rights of Jews was an integral aspect of the relation between colonizer and colonized.[65] A clear picture emerges in British imperial discourse of European powers as pledged to protect Jews as a common humanitarian enterprise, even if Jewish emancipation in Britain did not come until 1858.[66] At least in this period, European colonial enterprise among Muslim majority populations in the hinterland of the Ottoman lands thus became a site in which Jewish subjectivities were rendered as compatible with European civilization.

If Jews were largely accepted as European subjects in an imperial context, French and British writers both saw the Berber agriculturalists, especially the Kabyle peoples, as more prone to assimilation than the Arab population.[67] The American traveller George Ditson referred to them as the 'most troublesome and most interesting people in the country'.[68] He went on to argue that it was their 'susceptibility to civilization'—the evidence from their customs and habits that they could be assimilated as subjects—that made French plans to move them to reservations unnecessary and undesirable.[69] Warmsley, a military traveller, observed, 'Active, industrious, and intelligent . . . the Kabyle is essentially warlike, and though the various tribes fight among themselves, yet all unite against a common danger, forming a republic, which, up to the time of which I speak, had bid defiance to each successive race, which had swept as conquerors over Algeria'.[70] Similarly,

British Indian discourse on the Sikhs used the language of republicanism to understand them as egalitarian, warrior peasants. This use of a classical European analogy justified a more conciliatory policy on the part of the colonial administration.[71] Crucially, while the trope enabled a discourse on how such people were 'closer' to European models of civilization and thus could be governed more leniently, it also operated to imply an ineluctable division between European advancement and the archaic and stationary civilization of non-Europeans. At the same time, such descriptions reveal the general shift in British discourse on non-European or pre-commercial societies at this time away from the conjectural models of the Enlightenment toward a less schematic, more detailed approach to history and travel writing.[72]

The romantic register was appropriate for describing indigenous resistance to French rule precisely because it could present such acts as both honorable and futile in the face of progress. James Fenimore Cooper's *The Last of the Mohicans* and Sir Walter Scott's *Waverley* novels are only the most famous examples of this aspect of romanticism and modernity. The government established by Abd al-Qādir, his military resistance to the French, and eventual defeat inspired an outpouring of poems and panegyric biographies in Britain.[73] A notable early biography was by Charles Churchill, whose work was based on a series of interviews with Abd al-Qādir in Damascus. For Churchill, Abd al-Qādir's life was of interest because it was 'grand, ennobling and romantic', but his subject represented more than the last stand of an outmoded way of life.[74] As he wrote, 'To unite the Arabs of Algeria as one people, . . . to inspire them with patriotism, to call forth all their dormant capabilities, whether for war, for commerce, for agriculture, or for mental improvement; and then to crown the whole with the impress of European civilization—such was his might and comprehensive ideal'.[75] Churchill underscored Abd al-Qādir's effort to modernize his Arab polity. The book was dedicated to Napoleon III, whom Churchill praised for his gracious and honorable treatment of Abd al-Qādir. In this way, French imperial domain was vindicated as it honored its obligation to subject peoples as sanctioned by the surrender and acquiescence of noble leaders such as Abd al-Qādir. Churchill's account only added to an impression, particularly prevalent from the 1850s, that the Arab population could not assimilate and would be marginalized. 'The French,' Ellen Rogers wrote of Algiers, 'seem to do all they can to destroy the Eastern-looking aspect of the place, and gradually to pull down everything Moorish, around which Arab reminiscences are entwined'.[76] Protection rather than inclusion was all they could hope for. Rogers went on to write, 'The Arabs, not enjoying the privileges of French citizens, cannot fill any employment in the French administration; but their own manners, customs, and religion are protected by the Government'.[77] In this sense, the Arab population became an obstacle to the benefits of European imperial rule and, by the same logic, a justification for the consolidation of French control.

IV

I suggested earlier that three themes in British discourse on metropolitan France also emerged in discussion on Algeria. They were the reckless pursuit of political progress, the neglect of civil liberties, and the lack of material prosperity. Costly wars, truculent and assertive settlers, failed settlements, and the ungovernability of large groups of the population are common themes in all the material reviewed in this chapter. The American traveller George Ditson used a protestant language of progress to write, 'Steam and electricity are doing their wondrous work, they are levelling with the dust many of the degrading barriers of ancient customs and laws. They are throwing the light of knowledge rapidly and surely over the darkness of the East, so long in thraldom of the priesthood. They are the iconoclasts of the nineteenth century'.[78] But such optimism was uncommon in British discourse. This book has argued that a central concern of British discourse on French Algeria was the ambiguity of the legality, moral purpose, and administration of French Algeria.

The belief that France shared with Britain a common aim as liberal civilizing powers came increasingly under strain with the succession of the authoritarian Napoleon III. The British Empire offered few ready comparisons to the unprecedented spectacle of a burgeoning settler population among such a large, heterogeneous indigenous population with a string of sophisticated commercial ports. As we have seen, British discourse frequently contrasted the chaos and brutality of French Algerian rights regimes, policing and land distribution policies with those of the British Empire. While some looked to British precedent in evaluating French Algeria, others—such as Engels—emphasized and relished the novelty and decisiveness of this French imperial project.

The radical or progressive belief in the appropriateness of such actions for a civilized power was less common than disapproval. Such contemporary observations remind us that the violence and disorder of empire contrasted with or was disguised through a rhetoric of order and legalism. As has often been noted, Alexis de Tocqueville saw this as a hypocritical aspect of British imperialism, bemoaning 'their perpetual attempts to prove that they act in the interest of a principal, or for the good of the natives, or even for the advantages of the sovereigns they subjugate'.[79] As Lauren Benton has recently argued, the constitutional structures used for imperial domination make it often inappropriate to attempt to analyze empire as a state of exception or as the abuse of a constituted legal or moral order.[80] In this sense, British discourse on French Algeria confirms a general need in this period to give European imperial encounters an institutional, legal, and moral legitimacy that need not stem from reason of state or the pursuit of national glory. In his essay 'A Few Words on Non-Interference', John Stuart Mill observed of French Algeria, 'A civilized government cannot help having barbarous neighbours: when it has, it cannot always content itself with a defensive position, one of mere resistance to aggression. After a longer or shorter interval of forbearance, it either finds itself obliged to conquer them, or to assert so much authority over them, and so break their spirit, that they gradually sink into a state of dependence . . . [and then] it has become morally responsible for all evil it allows them to do'.[81] Mill's observation is significant because it explains why, regardless of whether they condoned or condemned the first phases of military conquest, all commentators saw France as obligated to the just government and good management of the peoples of Algeria.

This leads to the question of not simply how a diverse colonial society should be governed but how they are defined in relation to the colonial power and what rights can be conferred on them. This concern was evident in the descriptions outlined earlier of Jews, Kabyles, Arabs, and colonists as members of a colonial polity. Even in this period, Algeria provides an example of a pattern Rogers Brubaker has observed for France itself, namely that political inclusion has been seen to stem from cultural assimilation.[82] However, Brubaker's observations about metropolitan France do not go far enough for the context of invasion, conquest, and conflict in French Algeria. Inclusion, exclusion, and other categories stem from governability. Those groups who demonstrate themselves to be capable of being governed, depending on how well they have done this, take place within a hierarchy.[83] British discourse recognized this in policies toward the various peoples of French Algeria and in the standoff between the military government and the colonists. Exclusion seemed to operate differently in the two empires. In the British case, the issue was whether rights applied to different peoples (such as British subjects from Asian colonies, non-Anglicans, indigenous peoples and so on). In the French case, the issue became one of whether people were able to exercise those responsibilities that went with rights. Hence, with the sénatus-consulte of 1865, it became possible to become a full French citizen by renouncing one's Muslim personal code.[84] The Crémieux Declaration of 1870 conferred French citizenship to Algerian Jews without requiring them to renounce their personal code.[85] British observers noticed that a central aspect of the French imperial project in Algeria was the degree to which certain peoples were better able to become citizens, meaning acquiring the capacity to govern themselves to become active members of the polity. The historical context for these national discourses of citizenship is not simply the metropole, the colony, or the tension between the two. As in this case, it can also be those ambiguous sites where membership of a polity, the capacity to have rights, and the existence of rights were all constituted through the practice of empire.

The writings discussed here clearly form an element of a 'national' or 'imperial' tradition that was itself part of the competitive struggles between the British and the French to establish their own traditions or styles of citizenship, dominion, and imperium. That said, even if Edward Said is correct that 'imperialism was so globalizing that nothing escaped it', then it is clear that we still need an analytical framework to understand intra-European co-operative imperial projects and their role in constituting the European and the non-European.[86] This is especially the case when we study the emergence of discourses of citizenship formed in the context of empire. The perceived eligibility to claim rights in the first place is conferred by definitions of what attributes or actions give the capacity to do so. The assumptions as to why Jews but not Muslims could unconditionally be European British subjects or French citizens is a good example of this. If we are to identify the ways in which British, French, and European discourses of citizenship retain inequalities, bars, and restrictions fashioned through imperial experience, the pretense that each tradition is principally to be understood as mutually exclusive or oppositional should be put aside.

Chapter 5

Subjects across Empires

I

If imperial subjects had any rights at all, they were often only evident when moving between empires. In part this was because imperial or even national sovereignty only came into being in any practical sense when it was claimed or observed. The analysis of British discourse on Algeria examines how the French invasion reconstituted British imperial space in the Mediterranean. It provides a brief example of the ways in which the European political subject was constituted not simply in opposition to non-European colonial populations but also in the interplay of different European experiences of imperial domination.

A central concern of this chapter is how British political language and discursive traditions were formed by the reshaping of an imperial space. In the first half of the nineteenth century, the authority of the Deys of Algiers was challenged both locally and by British, French, and American naval incursions, culminating in the French invasion of 1830 and subsequent attempts to cement and extend France's control along the coast and into the interior of Algeria. The study of British engagement with Algeria reveals a focus on the groups of people who passed through and resided in the major ports along the coast. In doing so, it reveals the ways in which borders within and between sites of imperial domination were at times created by differentiations between rights-bearing subjects themselves rather than by territorial boundaries.[1] The formal division between 'British Subjects, Moors [and] persons who are Subjects of European Powers' in contemporary British consular records is a strong example of this.² As Lauren Benton has ably demonstrated for this period, the assertion of sovereignty is best recognized through the analysis of practices regarding the movements and regulation of people rather than formal metropolitan claims or predominantly institutional frameworks. This has been a fairly well studied aspect of legal pluralism and the exclusion of non-European or indigenous peoples from full citizenship rights.³ Yet the presence of Britons in French Algeria raises questions about how subjects were constituted legally, how European subjects in non-European lands claimed and lost extraterritorial privileges, and, most importantly, the limits of ethno-linguistic or even racial definitions of who could be a subject in the context of the nineteenth century. As will be seen the vast majority of 'British subjects' in Algeria were Maltese or Jews from Gibraltar. Equally, British observers were only too aware that demographics left the French reliant on colonists from Spain, Malta, Italy, and Portugal to form a French citizenry in Algeria.⁴ In other words, Algeria provides an example of imperial subject identities, normally associated with people from or in the metropole, being conferred on those who, but for the colonial context, would otherwise be on the margins of or excluded from the enjoyment of such rights and obligations.

The ways in which the rights of British subjects in Algeria were enacted provide an insight into how imperial territories worked in practice in the early nineteenth century. As the next section argues, this demonstrates the ascendency of diplomatic and political practice over formal principles of international law or the close adherence to treaties. Legal language and reference to norms and treaty obligations were important. However, as the succeeding section shows, they were given form by the interpretations of diplomats on the ground negotiating between the directives of the Foreign and Colonial Offices at home on the one hand and shifting local politics on the other. The Consul records reveal a confluence between shifting imperial power politics, local rivalries, the ebb and flow of populations across the region and the individual lives of the people who sought or received Consular protection. Viewing the British imperial subject on all these different scales at once is useful for seeing fully how this status was constructed. The focus on the movement of people and borders encourages a vision of individual empires that takes note of the role of other empires, local politics, and global commerce as related but distinct drivers of the practice of imperial subjecthood.

II

The movement of British subjects across the shifting imperial territories of the Mediterranean provides insights into many aspects of subjecthood and European empires in a period that combined a growing imperial presence in key regions such as the Mediterranean with an impetus for economic migration. In the early nineteenth century, British commentators and diplomats evoked a range of sources, from treatises on international law to treaties and common practice, in an effort to establish how to make sense of such shifts in territory and population. A number of issues came into play.

The idea of a law of nations which regulated practices between sovereign nations was tempered by a sense that interactions between European or Christian nations required a different set of norms to those between European and non-European nations. There was a lack of consensus among European theorists of international law in the early Modern period. If the non-Christian Barbary States along the North African coast, including Algiers, were regarded as full nations in a natural law sense, then any treaties with them were between equal partners. If they were not deemed civilized and therefore not full nations, then such treaties were merely instruments of policy.[5] This mattered because it lessened the obligation on the civilized powers to be bound by treaties. As the leading scholar of the history of international law, C. H. Alexandrowicz has observed, such ambiguity makes the court decisions of the period all the more important. In the case of the Barbary States, a number of important rulings in English courts in the late eighteenth and early nineteenth century confirmed that while certain norms and practices existed between all nations, these states did not adhere to the same laws between nations as Christian nations. For some commentators such as the American jurist and diplomat Henry Wheaton, the diplomatic practices of the Barbary States and of the Ottoman Empire more generally pointed to use of the international legal practices of Christian nations, including those regarding the ransom of prisoners and treatment of ambassadors.[6] As recent scholarship has underscored, actual practice was characterized by inconsistent use of a range of sources and precedents.[7] Political expediency and use of a set of clear norms and rules were not clearly separated. This was particularly the case during the first decades of the nineteenth century in the Mediterranean as power and influence shifted between the larger imperial powers, namely the French, British, and Ottoman empires.

What can be said of the places that imperial subjects moved through and where they claimed rights and protections? From the late eighteenth century through the Napoleonic Wars, these territories had changed both through conquest and treaty negotiation. In the space of fifty years, sovereignty over the island of Malta had transferred from the Knights of St. John to the French, and then to the British. As Julia Clancy-Smith has noted, such shifts of nominal sovereignty affected not only the territories that change hands but also those areas that neighbor them.[8] Clancy-Smith's evocation of nearby Tunisia as a borderland captures this well. Patterns of migration, commerce, and local political control were deeply affected by such changes. In this period in particular, Maltese and Ionian subjects of the British Empire could be found across the Mediterranean. Spanish, Italian, and French economic migrants moved around the area, particularly along the North African coast. Settler colonial migration narratives about the anglophone world have been researched extensively both on a national and transnational scale.[9] As a range of historians of the Mediterranean and of nineteenth-century migration have argued, narratives of the mix of populations and of territories in the Mediterranean have been elided by national or even nationalist historiographies.[10] Equally, studies of individual groups such as Jews in the Mediterranean have been possible largely because these categories and movements appear in colonial and national archives.[11] The study of how such groups are described or constituted in the archival record is essential to any history of the rights and protections of mobility that make up imperial subjecthood.

III

The British presence in Algeria in the first decades of French conquest had deep implications not only for the question of who a British subject was but also how the subjects of one European power were to be treated in the imperial domain of another. The British were part of a European and a Christian presence in Algeria. This was reinforced by an awareness of local Muslim legal and political practices which reinforced this division. The French invasion realigned this relationship. It redefined and placed new constraints on British imperial enterprise as embodied in the presence of its subjects in a non-European territory.

The French invasion of Algeria was understood by contemporaries as an act of aggrandizement in a politically unstable but economically and militarily important region. Anglo-French relations were guided by a mutual desire to avoid war but shaped by rivalry in the Middle East, North Africa, and the Caribbean.[12] The perceived weakness of the Ottoman Empire created numerous flashpoints. Some led to cooperation, for example over the Crimean War in the 1850s. Others created suspicion and discord, such as the British abolition of slavery in 1833 (fifteen years before the French) or French support for Ali Pasha against the Ottomans in Egypt. In the years before the invasion, this tension was in evidence along the coast of what would become Algeria. Longstanding agreements with the Dey of Algiers and other local rulers to protect shipping had broken down as the Dey's power waned. The threat to western shipping had prompted the first U.S. naval expedition outside of American waters, earning the Americans most favored nation status with the Dey in 1815.[13] At the time of the French invasion, both France and Britain were angling to displace the United States and to protect their commercial interests on the crumbling periphery of the Ottoman Empire. The joint British and Dutch bombardment of Algiers in 1816, led by Lord Exmouth, had ended in an agreement to end the enslavement of Europeans. French blockades from 1827 onward and the eventual invasion in 1830 gave France an ascendency. However, even as late as 1831, the British Consul of Algiers noted, 'We might make this the finest country in the world in a very short time & the natives know this, and wish for our dominion here'.[14] In other words, Anglo-French cooperation in the region was never entirely to be assumed. In part, this was because continued local political volatility meant that the territorial control and influence of the competing imperial powers was not seen to be fixed.

A sense of common interest as Christian powers in a land characterized by disorder and social and political decay marked relations between Britain and France in the region.[15] More generally, European diplomatic connections with the ports of northern Algeria continued to focus on protecting shipping from piracy and paying ransoms to local political groupings. It is interesting to note that the invasion by the French created further uncertainty because their influence did not spread far beyond a narrow strip of the coast. During the 1830s, various nongovernment groups, notably the Company of Ironmongers of the City of London, attempted to establish independent agents, funded by subscription, for negotiating the release of prisoners.[16] The Consul expressed concern to London that it was often unclear until after the prisoners had been rescued whether the individuals were British subjects or not. It was acknowledged that Britain's obligation to Christians generally mitigated this problem.[17] This sense of common cause was emphasized in a letter from the secretary of state at the Colonial Office to the British Consul regarding a dispute over the use of the Christian cemetery in Algiers. As he wrote, 'I trust between you and your fellow consuls, [you] will succeed in righting the disturbance of that harmony and good will which ought especially to prevail among Christians whom circumstances may have brought into one small community in a Mahomedan Country'.[18] Many writers took the opportunity to depict the French as new crusaders against the crescent. Henry Reeve writing in the *Edinburgh Review* called the French invasion a renewal of the 'ancient combat of the Crescent and the Cross'.[19] Reeve was writing as an expert on French colonial policy. A Whig man of letters, he frequently reviewed works on contemporary politics, France, and the Near East for the *Edinburgh Review* and was the main English translator of the works of French statesman Alexis de Tocqueville. The use of such tropes reinforced a sense of common Christian interest arising from a flux in local geopolitical relationships along the North African coast.

Crucially, British subjects in Algeria were an ethnically heterogeneous group, including a large number of protected persons or *protégés*. According to the official return for 1838, Bône and Algiers had the largest concentrations of British subjects with 1,135 and 988, respectively. It was believed that the vast majority of these were Maltese.[20] The same return also records the protestant population of Algiers to be 211, compared to over 12,000 Muslims, 5,000 Catholics, and 6,000 Jews. The consular records reveal that ensuring the provision of protestant rites in the Christian cemetery formed a regular part of the consul's activities.[21] While British subjects were officially prohibited from serving in the armies of enemies of the French, examples can be found. The most prominent was Colonel Scott, a mercenary in Abd al-Qādir's forces fighting against the French, who published a memoir. By the end of our period, Algiers was emerging as a popular wintering destination—memoirs such as Ellen Rogers's *A Winter in Algeria* are representative of this trend.

As the Consular records show, the flow of British subjects to Algiers reflected population pressures elsewhere in the Mediterranean, particularly overcrowding in Malta and Gibraltar.[22] From the time of the Dey of Algiers and into the period of French occupation, merchants and trade continued to be the most important aspect of the British presence, at least from the point of view of the British consul. In 1831, the British Consul of Algiers was prompted to complain about this to the British authorities in Gibraltar. He noted that the authorities in Gibraltar seemed to want to encourage 'foreign subjects' to go to Algiers instead. 'Algiers', he stated, 'is crowded with hundreds of people who have come here to seek employment & cannot get a livelihood, on which account I should think it advisable to let this be known to such of the inhabitants of Gibraltar who may be led into the error of quitting the garrison for this country'.[23] As will be seen regarding the Greek War of Independence and British protection of subjects of the Ionian Islands, there was a link between the management of British colonial possessions in the Mediterranean and the flow of British subjects to other parts of the region.

IV

If claiming the protection of their government is a major way in which subjects constitute themselves, the records of the Consul of Algiers provide a lucid picture of how this process was shaped by Britain's global presence. Before exploring the ways in which protection was rendered, it is worth reflecting on the efforts the Consul made to be able to assert British authority and offer protection. For example, in 1827, at the beginning of animosity between the French and the Dey, reports of a buildup of French troops led the Consul to request firearms from the Chief Secretary of Gibraltar. The reason he gave was concern about possible ensuing disorder and unrest. As he wrote, 'in the event of a French invasion we should have much to fear from the Arabs & other Armed people form the Country'.[24] As tensions heightened between the Dey and the French, the Consul secured British naval protection. In August 1829, he wrote to the commander of HMS *Pelorus*, 'The negotiations between the Dey of Algiers and the French Commodore having been broken off, under circumstances which will probably compel the latter to attack Algiers either by land or by sea, I am under the necessity in conformity to my instructions from the Secretary of State to call on you for such protection as may be in your power to afford me'.[25] As he went on to note, 'In the case of a mere Bombardment the Dey gives me assurances (in which place confidence) that the Christians will be protected by some of his troops allotted for that purpose . . . as the Arabs & Cabyles may take advantage of the confusion to attack our house for purposes of pillage—however I am in little fear of such an event if only an attack by sea is mediated, and the sight of a British flag in the offing would be a stronger protection than the Dey can afford'.[26] The nexus of local arrangements, British naval support, and diplomatic protection was essential to the continuance of consulates such as that in Algiers; also, as these examples show, it required negotiation both with local authorities and a range of fellow British administrators to secure resources and assurances.

Trade was one of the most common areas where government protection applied. Writing in 1829 about the requisition of goods by the Dey of Algiers from a Greek ship flying a British flag, the Consul confirmed the importance of this protection. As he explained, 'The loss of this property from under the British flag in time of peace caused considerable sensation here at the time, amongst all classes of people as the British flag was always the most preferred and depended upon here. And on this account, I am particularly anxious that we should get it restored if possible, in order to reestablish the credit of our shipping on this Coast'.[27] As will be seen, the loss by the British of key trading privileges following the French invasion was a major cause of concern. The performance of protection—which came at a high cost—was a means of asserting British power in a foreign context.

The release of prisoners and the payment of ransoms remained prominent aspects of consular activity before and after the French invasion. Significantly, these practices point to the fragile and shifting political control across the Mediterranean. For example, in 1828, during the Greek War of Independence from the Ottomans, the Consul expressed concern that three Greek prisoners of war—British *protégés*—were being held as slaves. This contravened an agreement between the British and the Dey of Algiers, 'in which he declares that all Prisoners of War shall be trusted with humanity and not treated as slaves until regularly exchanged according to the usage of European Powers'.[28] The continued payment of ransoms to tribes and other groups for the release of British and other European subjects reflected the limited territorial authority that the Dey of Algiers and then the French had beyond a stretch of the coast.[29] In 1834, the Colonial Office made it clear that negotiation was a key aspect of the Consul's role. The Consul was reminded that 'you must contrive to effect his ransom on the most economical terms'.[30] Struggle for territorial control continued to involve the capture of British subjects. In 1840, the Consul reported that a number of Maltese had been captured by Abd al-Qādir's forces in his sustained resistance to French control.[31]

Most British subjects in Algiers and along the coast were either Jewish merchants born or long-time residents in Gibraltar or Maltese subjects. As Catholics and Jews, such individuals would have enjoyed the same rights as any British subject abroad, while in practice they would have faced many barriers to the full enjoyment of the civil and political rights of British subjects in the metropole. Malta had been a British protectorate since 1800 and a Crown Colony since 1813. As the consular records show, intervening in commercial disputes and criminal matters were common aspects of this protection. Another common feature was to do with civil rights particularly relating to births, deaths, and marriages. In 1840, the Consul wrote to the British authorities in Malta regarding the implication of a lack of documentation for a Maltese subject. He wrote, 'Great difficulties constantly arise here from the Maltese not being provided with the Certificate of their Baptism and Marriage. And at this moment a Maltese is unable to get his child baptized in consequence of his having no proof of his marriage with the mother, which is insisted on by the Mayor previous to its registration & subsequent baptism'.[32]

The question of which individuals would be subject to British protection was particularly significant in the case of protection of Jews. Throughout this period, the Consul frequently expressed dismay at the ambiguity of passports issued in Gibraltar. This issue was exasperated during this period as the government of Gibraltar attempted to reduce the number of British subjects by increasing the eligibility threshold.[33] The lack of uniformity or central control in this respect is evident from the circulars that were frequently sent to consuls from London requesting information on what rules were being applied by consulates in the issuing of passports.[34] Some passports stated that the bearer was a

'Resident' but it was unclear whether they were a British subject.[35] As he wrote, 'I think it would save much trouble if you were to insert the words British Subjects in the Passports of those who are so, as the title of "Inhabitant of Gibraltar" does not imply that the bearer has resided there long enough to become a Denizen of that place'.[36] The Consul went on to note, 'Of course every person bringing a British Passport will be protected by us, even if not strictly entitled to the privileges of a British Subject, privately tho' I should wish to avoid any public question arising with this Government, unless the evidence I could produce should be quite incontestable'.[37] As this correspondence shows, much of the problem arose because the British Consul felt obliged to appear to be offering full protection.

During this period, the need to be seen to act shaped British policy toward the Jews claiming protection by virtue of birth or long-time residence in Gibraltar. The Don Pacifico case (1847–1850), in which a Jewish merchant acting as Portuguese Consul in Greece was able to claim the protection of the British government through his birth in Gibraltar, is usually understood in terms of Foreign Secretary Lord Palmerston's cynical assertion of British preeminence. Yet the protection of Jews has recently been described as a fifth pillar of British imperial expansion in this period, alongside free trade, utilitarianism, Evangelical Christianity, and antislavery.[38] It is significant that, at least in the Mediterranean, the frontier of British imperial interest was constituted not by territory alone, but by people; not by subjects that asserted racial or ethnic ideals of British-ness, but by those who would have faced de facto and de jure restrictions on their civil and political rights when located in the metropole.[39]

The invasion was followed by years of uncertainty about French intentions and about their ability to control their territory. The British Consul worked within this liminal and shifting political context. For example, in the early 1830s, the French decided not to replace the Governor of Oran, a major port west of Algiers. Confusion ensued. In 1834, the Consul wrote to the Governor of Oran about a number of claims to property from British subjects. As he wrote, 'The [British] Vice Consul at Oran having reported to me that he cannot get justice at your hands, alleging that the French Commandant prevents you & checks you in the experience of your authority, I have seen the General In Chief who showed me his letter to the French Commandant at Oran forbidding him to interfere in the civil administration'.[40] Such confusion created a need to work with multiple powerbrokers. This can be seen as well in the continued British negotiations with tribes along the coast and in the interior for the release of British subjects. In this sense, the French invasion's reshaping of imperial space was partial and complex in its operation.

One major change brought about by the French invasion was that British subjects moved from being Europeans under a non-European (specifically Muslim) government to being within a European regime. Preferential shipping rights—a key advantage for merchants operating under a British flag—could no longer be enforced, and, as the secretary of state acknowledged, the British could do nothing about this under international law.[41] Four years later, the Colonial Office confirmed to the Consul that he no longer had the right to be present when a British ship was searched by the authorities in Algiers.[42] British subjects lost extraterritorial protection from local jurisdiction that they had enjoyed under the Dey.[43] They also lost the right to permanently own land. As the Colonial Office acknowledged in this case, 'The laws of all European nations interdict to Foreigners a permanent tenure of lands or other removable property'.[44] In 1835, the amended civil code stated that foreigners 'admitted to the enjoyment of civil rights' could be required to serve in the National Guard.[45] As the legal counsel of Britain's Ambassador to France observed, any British subject engaging in commerce would be deemed to be enjoying civil rights.[46] The point in all these cases is that British subjects in Algeria lost the privileges they enjoyed under Ottoman rule and were understood to now be bound by the law as it pertained among European nations. Through the invasion, Algeria thus became both a European legal space and a mutable and changing site for the administration of indigenous legal practices. This is the context in which the presence in Algeria of British observers and the observations of the various writers sampled in this article should be understood.

V

The British consulate in Algiers is just one example among many of how the protection of subjects worked in this period. It provides a rare insight into inter-imperial relations, particularly into how changes in local rule reconstituted the British imperial presence itself. As this chapter has shown, that presence was not simply about the movement of individuals. Crucially, it was about the legal and political tools that were employed—from ransoming to enforcing civil and commercial contracts—to provide British protection. Four main observations can be made.

First, the period under study witnessed a shift in territorial sovereignty in Algiers that reframed the British consular presence. What began as an outpost in a non-European space became part of a web of British diplomatic posts within a fellow European empire. This led to a change in treaty obligations but also in norms. Crucially, coming firmly within the ambit of a fellow European power reduced the freedom to operate above and outside local laws. This reconstitution of the British imperial presence points to the ways in which histories of the various western empires are imbricated not only with each other but also with those of non-European powers. This is true of the history of empires but also of the imperial subjects that moved within and between them.

Secondly, this chapter reveals how shifting power relationships affected populations within the region and therefore how colonial populations were governed beyond as well as within imperial borders. As Valeska Huber, Julia Clancy-Smith, and many others have shown, the Mediterranean in this period was a complex array of patterns of economic migration. The significant political destabilization of the first half of the nineteenth century combined not only with substantial overcrowding in Mediterranean territories, such as Malta, but also across much of Europe led to large waves of migration southward to the northern coast of Africa. Some of this was local, as can be seen by the volume of British consular business relating to the French invasion. Other impacts were more indirect—for example, the way in which the Greek War of Independence displaced populations and affected shipping patterns in the central and western Mediterranean, resulting in new demands on the Consul.

Thirdly, this case sheds light on the role of what came to be known as humanitarian concerns in the shaping of how British protection operated. This can be seen in the case of the Maltese, Gibraltarian Jewish, and Greek subjects under British protection. In many instances, including where Jews were concerned, policy was articulated in terms of obligations on Britain as a Christian power protecting religious rites in majority Muslim territories. Domestically, British rule in Malta entailed a Protestant power protecting and preserving the rights of a

Catholic people. Humanitarian language was pertinent to activities freeing slaves. Of course, this also had a clear commercial aspect, as much of it related to the protection of individuals employed on ships or in enterprises flying British flags. As we have seen from the consular correspondence, the use of British passports and the British flag for shipping brought considerable commercial gains. These could only be secured if British protection was seen to be active and effective.

This leads to a fourth element: the importance of British protection as a means of promoting British commerce. The British presence in Algiers and the kinds of activities in which it was involved reflected the centrality of trade as a motive for furnishing protection so consistently and so thoroughly. This matters because it affected the kinds of rights that were enforced, such as those relating to commercial contracts, the ownership of property, and the protection of British subjects travelling through the region. Also relevant is the question of who was protected. As the correspondence shows, uncertainty about identifying legitimate claims to belonging to a particular group was a recurrent problem. In part this was because the British already assumed that they would be taking an expansive view of who was entailed to such protection. As the Don Pacifico case and the 'gun-boat diplomacy' that it typified suggest, the performance of protection was as important as or more important than who was actually being protected.

The role of commercial and military considerations in shaping the imperial subjecthood has always been clear in the large body of scholarship on the operation of empire within colonial and metropolitan studies. These considerations operate differently beyond the borders of empire. In these contexts, commercial and military factors are more obviously tempered by international laws and norms and the presence of other powers. This chapter's focus on the movement of people and borders encourages a vision of individual empires that takes note of the role of other empires, local politics, and global commerce. It brings out their role as related but distinct drivers of the practice of imperial subjecthood. These practices and their regulation are an instructive forerunner of the contemporary citizenship regime in the context of globalization.

Conclusion

Modern citizenship remains heavily marked by its colonial origins. Mid-twentieth-century decolonization was only a partial rupture. Contemporary efforts to 'decolonize' institutions, from universities to banks, suggest that this is the case. We continue to be confronted with evidence of racial, ethnic, and religious inequalities woven into the institution of citizenship in former colonies such as India and former colonial powers such as Britain. It is tempting to see the problems of citizenship today as having immediate causes. As we discussed in chapters 1 and 3, much recent writing on citizenship in Britain and France assumes that increased levels of immigration from former colonies put unbearable strain on national culture and national institutions in Britain and France. Through a range of examples, I have indicated that these tensions within citizenship are not new. They are inherited from empire. This is not simply in terms of creating colonial populations with an expectation that they have a place in contemporary Britain and France. More importantly, this is the inheritance of empire because modern, supposedly 'national' citizenship regimes have repressive features that originate in empire.

I have considered three main examples in this book. Chapter 2 examined how supposed liberal freedoms could be claimed in unfree colonial societies. A clear binary between a rules-based liberal metropole and the authoritarian government of a colony—British India—may have been the aspiration of some British colonial administrators, but significant groups within colonial society itself demonstrated a desire to claim rights, to shape what it meant to be a British subject. This moves the history of 'western ideas' beyond the geographical focus of the west and demonstrates the limits of colonial control in the face of rights claiming. Chapter 4 shows how the French invasion of Algeria was understood as a colonial act by British audiences. This gives an insight into how writers and commentators from the metropole analyzed how colonial rule worked. Crucially, it reveals a key feature of colonial rule, the identifying and managing of groups within the population—religious and ethnic, for example. 'European settlers' were also one of the groups to be managed in this schema. Building on this, chapter 5 explored how imperial subjects claimed rights through travelling in other realms. The politics of mobility is arguably one of the most important aspects of the contemporary citizenship regime, and this chapter attempts to unearth something of its colonial history. These instances do not create a comprehensive picture of the colonial roots of modern citizenship, but they do expose a long and complex history of the role of identity creation, rights claiming, and mobility. Put another way, they enable a reading of colonial history as part of the story of the origins of national citizenship regimes.

A number of themes are worth emphasizing regarding the role of the colonial in national citizenship formation in the nineteenth century. Both British India and French Algeria point to the limitations of colonial settlers as carriers of European civilization in the view of metropolitan commentators at this time. The settler colonies provide an essential focus for discussions of autonomy, gender, class, national identity, and race as integral aspects of the metropolitan history of democratization and citizenship in British and French thought. For British and French administrators and metropolitan observers of French Algeria for instance, the colonists failed to demonstrate full capacity as responsible rights-bearing Europeans. Becoming a colonist, law abiding and law giving, required discipline in the form of government regulation. As Julia Clancy-Smith has argued for North Africa, the story of European settlers in this vast region is elided by other historiographers, mostly national. The same is true of the frustrated attempts to promote European colonization of British India in the 1820s and 1830s. Other narratives of settler colonies exist but they contend with the fact that a settler population has remained and become dominant, for example in Canada or Australia. The examples discussed in this work aim to provide a wide perspective on the ways in which settler colonies were a site of experimentation with European rights claiming and belonging that is complementary to the history of how national citizenship took shape in metropolitan contexts such as Britain and France.

The central concern of this book has mostly been about forms of civil rights claims and aspects of colonial governance in British India, French Algeria, and the British and French Algeria. However, there is so much more to this story. Violence and repression, so well documented in a still expanding body of scholarship, were prominent features of colonial rule and remain aspects of this legacy, both in terms of historic memory and the structure of contemporary institutions. Equally important is the partial, ad hoc, and inconsistent reach of colonial government. Scholars such as John Darwin and Lauren Benton have pointed to the frequent failure of colonial rule to have an impact beyond certain centers of power, such as urban areas or garrisons. The example of the British presence in French Algeria points to the partial and inconsistent exercise of imperial authority and the way in which power was exercised differently at different levels. As we saw, colonial power was not demonstrated or exercised by the central administration of policy as much as by local contingencies.

As a status, a formal collection of rights and obligations, citizenship is limited and limiting. Its force and meaning are negotiated but also unstable. Much of this book has been concerned with rights or ways of being political that would come to be seen as aspects of the history of citizenship, even if they were not understood in this way at the time. One can easily overstate the significance of resemblances and analogies between the historical formation of citizenship and its manifestation today. My aim in this book has been to question a key assumption about the historical conditions that shape contemporary citizenship, namely that its origins are situated within European, largely national regimes. This is a question of geographic specificity. As chapter 1 suggested, citizenship has been seen as a European institution imported elsewhere. This view has been a feature of both standard western political narratives and their postcolonial critiques. I argue that contemporary national, or even 'western' citizenship has been significantly shaped by the experience of colonialism.

This leads to my second point. Aspects of citizenship such as its precarity and its use as a tool not only of exclusion but also of subordination are as much a part of its history as rights claiming and the performance of obligations. The idea that forms of colonial violence prefigure the age of totalitarianism in Europe in the 1930s and 1940s was a central tenet of Hannah Arendt's *Origins of Totalitarianism* (1951). Arendt's particular interest was the immediate origins of forms of violence and extermination that emerged in the high imperialism of the late nineteenth century. The present in which she wrote was the era immediately after World War II. How do we make sense of citizenship in contemporary Europe? To answer such a question, a wider range of forms of control and domination must be considered. We must also, I would suggest, fully reject the assumption that Europe colonialism and citizenship have parallel, mostly separate histories up to the twentieth century. This book has offered a few examples of how we might write a longer, interwoven history of the multiple lives of European citizenship and European colonialism.

This has implications for how research is conducted on contemporary citizenship and its historic formation. I am confident in stating that it shows the need for greater dialogue between historians and social scientists. The historian contemplating what makes up citizenship has a more complex task than closely contextualizing the use of the term 'citizen'. The historical formation of various elements that came to be called citizenship is the object of study in describing and analyzing imperial citizenship. What matters here is not the contextual specificity of the name but the historical circumstance that created the forms of belonging, repertoires of action, and mechanisms of regulation that we associate with contemporary citizenship.

If citizenship is seen as vulnerable and mutable, such features are best understood over time. Social scientists have no choice but to become historians of the present as contemporary events relentlessly show. Crucially, studying that history is not a question of 'unearthing facts' but interrogating the vision of the past and makes up any citizenship regime in the present. How the past is perceived informs the study of certain defining features of modern citizenship. Both the taking away and the claiming of rights point to the fragility of what it means to be a citizen.

Notes

INTRODUCTION

1. Hannah Arendt, *Origins of Totalitarianism* (New York: Houghton Mifflin Harcourt, 1985), 126.
2. Ibid., 138.
3. Ibid., 127–29.
4. See, for example, Bernard Porter, *The Absent-Minded Imperialists: Empire, Society, and Culture in Britain* (Oxford: Oxford University Press, 2004), 1–10. For a counter-argument, see John M. MacKenzie, ' "Comfort" and "Conviction": A Response to Bernard Porter', in *The Journal of Imperial and Commonwealth History*, Vol. 36, No. 4 (2008): 659–68.
5. J. Evans, P. Grimshaw, D. Philips, and S. Swain, *Equal Subjects, Unequal Rights: Indigenous Peoples in British Settler Colonies 1830–1910* (Manchester: Manchester University Press, 2003); Catherine Hall, *Civilising Subjects: Metropole and Colony in the English Imagination, 1830–1867* (London: Polity, 2002).
6. Olivier Le Coeur Grandmaison, *Exterminer. Coloniser Sur la guerre et l'Etat colonial* (Paris: Fayard, 2005), 2–10; Anthony Anghie, *Imperialism, Sovereignty and the Making of International Law* (Cambridge: Cambridge University Press, 2004), 53–57.

CHAPTER 1

1. Walter Mignolo, 'The Geopolitics of Knowledge and the Colonial Difference', *The South Atlantic Quarterly*, Winter (2002): 67.

2. For the history of the Decree, see John Ruedy, *Modern Algeria* (Bloomington: Indiana University Press, 2005), 77.

3. Patrick Weill, *How to Be a French Citizen* (Durham, NC: Duke University Press, 2008), 128.

4. Gérard Noiriel, *The French Melting Pot: Immigration, Citizenship and French Identity*, trans. Geoffroy De Lafocarde (Minneapolis: University of Minnesota Press, 1996), 261.

5. Pap Ndiaye, *La condition noire: Essai sur une minorité française* (Paris: Broché, 2009), 286, 305.

6. Jacques Derrida, *The Monolingualism of the Other, or The Prosthesis of Origin*, trans. Patrick Mensah (Stanford, CA: Stanford University Press, 1998), 16.

7. Amelia Gentleman, 'The Week That Took Windrush from Low-Profile Investigation to National Scandal', *The Guardian*, 18 April 2018.

8. For a recent discussion of the longer history of the entrenched racial inequalities of both imperial subjecthood and contemporary British citizenship, see Catherine Hall, 'Mother Country', *London Review of Books*, Vol. 42, No. 2 (2020): 11–14; for studies of the racial aspects of post-1945 British migration and citizenship policy, see Kathleen Paul, *Whitewashing Britain: Race and Citizenship in the Postwar Era* (Ithaca, NY: Cornell University Press, 1997); Joe Turner, 'Internal Colonisation: The Intimate Circulations of Empire, Race and Liberal Government', *European Journal of International Relations*, Vol. 24, No. 4 (2018): 765–90.

9. Michael Freeden and Andrew Vincent, 'Introduction', in *Comparative Political Thought: Theorizing Practices*, eds. Michael Freeden and Andrew Vincent (London: Routledge, 2013), 20.

10. Paul Magnette, *Citizenship: The History of an Idea* (Colchester: ECPR, 2005); Derek Heater, *What Is Citizenship?* (London: John Wiley & Sons, 1999).

11. Bronwen Manby, *Citizenship and Statelessness in Africa: The Law and Politics of Belonging* (Oisterwijk: Wolf Legal Publishing, 2015), 9–11.

12. Richard J. Evans, 'The Demented Dalek', *London Review of Books*, Vol. 41, No. 17 (12 September 2019): 15.

13. Loi n° 2005–158 du 23 février 2005 portant reconnaissance de la Nation et contribution nationale en faveur des Français rapatriés.

14. Adrian Favell, *Philosophies of Integration Immigration and the Idea of Citizenship in France and Britain* (London: Palgrave Macmillan, 1998), 60.

15. Rahul Rao, *Third World Protest* (Oxford: Oxford University Press, 2010), 137.

16. Gayatri Chakravorty Spivak, *Outside in the Teaching Machine* (London: Routledge, 1993), 281.

17. Duncan Ivison, 'Justice and Imperialism: On the Very Idea of a Universal Standard', in *Law and Politics in British Colonial Thought: Transpositions*

of Empire, eds. Shaunnagh Dorsett and Ian Hunter (Basingstoke: Palgrave Macmillan, 2010).

18. Boaventura de Sousa Santos, *Epistemologies of the South: Justice against Epistemicide* (Boulder, CO: Paradigm Publishing, 2014).

19. For a recent debate on this, see Rosie Warren (ed.), *The Debate on Postcolonial Theory and the Spectre of Capital* (London: Verso, 2017).

20. John Darwin, *After Tamerlane: The Global History of Empire* (London: Penguin, 2007), 228.

21. Prominent examples include Christopher Bayly, *The Birth of the Modern World: Global Connections and Comparisons* (London: John Wiley & Sons, 2004); Erez Manela, *The Wilsonian Moment: Self-Determination and the International Origins of Anticolonial Nationalism* (London: Oxford University Press, 2007).

22. Heater, ibid.

23. Engin Isin, *Being Political: Genealogies of Citizenship* (London: University of Minnesota Press, 2002), xi.

24. Étienne Balibar, *We, The People of Europe?: Reflections on Transnational Citizenship* (Princeton, NJ: Princeton University Press, 2004), 87; Paul Gilroy, *After Empire: Postcolonial: Melancholia or Convivial Culture?* (London: Routledge, 2004), 85; Engin Isin and Peter Nyers, 'Introduction: Globalizing Citizenship Studies', in *Routledge Handbook of Citizenship Studies*, eds. Engin Isin and Peter Nyers (London: Routledge, 2014).

25. Jon Wilson, *Domination of Strangers: Modern Governance in Eastern India, 1780–1830* (London: Palgrave Macmillan, 2008), 15.

26. Cooper, *Citizenship between Empire and Nation: Remaking France and French Africa* (Princeton, NJ: Princeton University Press, 2014), 5.

27. Anthony Anghie, *Imperialism, Sovereignty and the Making of International Law* (Cambridge: Cambridge University Press, 2004), 38.

28. Wilson, *Domination of Strangers*, ibid.

29. For this critique of Said, see Arshin Adib-Moghaddam, *A Metahistory of the Clash of Civilisations: Us and Them beyond Orientalism* (Oxford: Oxford University Press, 2011), 88.

30. Richard Drayton, 'Where Does the World Historian Write From? Objectivity, Moral Conscience and the Past and Present of Imperialism', *Journal of Contemporary History*, Vol. 46, No. 3 (2011): 671–85.

31. Jeremy Adelman, 'What Is Global History?', *Aeon*, 2 March 2017. https://aeon.co/essays/is-global-history-still-possible-or-has-it-had-its-moment.

32. Eduardo Mendieta, 'Freedom as Practice and Civic Genius: On James Tully's Public Philosophy', in *Freedom and Democracy in an Imperial Context*, eds. Robert Nichols and Jakeet Singh (Abingdon: Routledge, 2014), 34.

33. Saliha Belmessous, *Assimilation and Empire: Uniformity in French and British Colonies, 1541–1954* (Oxford: Oxford University Press, 2014),

179–201; Faisal Devji, 'Apologetic Modernity', *Modern Intellectual History*, Vol. 4, No. 1 (2007): 61–76.

34. Engin Isin, 'Theorizing Acts of Citizenship', in *Acts of Citizenship*, eds. Engin Isin and Greg Nielsen (Chicago: University of Chicago Press, 2008), 20.

35. Isin, *Being Political*, 30.

36. Isin and Nyers, 'Globalizing Citizenship Studies', 6.

37. A notable exception is Elaine Hadley, *Living Liberalism: Practical Citizenship in Mid-Victorian Britain* (Chicago: University of Chicago Press, 2010).

38. Will Kymlicka, *Multicultural Citizenship: A Liberal Theory of Minority Rights* (Oxford: Oxford University Press, 1995); James Tully, *Public Philosophy in a New Key*, Vol. 1 (Cambridge: Cambridge University Press, 2008).

39. Rahul Rao, *Third World Protest: Between Home and the World* (Oxford: Oxford University Press, 2010), 44; Kumari Jayawardena, *Feminism and Nationalism in the Third World* (London: Zed Books, 1986).

40. See, for example, James Ferguson, *Anti-Politics Machine: Development, Depoliticization, and Bureaucratic Power in Lesotho* (Minneapolis: University of Minnesota Press, 1994), 67.

41. Quentin Skinner, 'Two Concepts of Citizenship', in *Tijdschrift voor Filosofie* 55ste Jaarg., Nr. 3 (1993): 404.

42. Hannah Weiss Muller, *Subjects and Sovereign: Bonds of Belonging in the Eighteenth Century British Empire* (Oxford: Oxford University Press, 2017), 4.

43. Rebecca Hartkopf Schloss, *Sweet Liberty: The Final Days of Slavery in Martinque* (Philadelphia: University of Pennsylvania Press, 2009); Julia Phillips Cohen, *Becoming Ottomans* (Oxford: Oxford University Press, 2014); Lauren Benton and Lisa Ford, *Rage for Liberty: The British Empire and the Origins of International Law* (Cambridge, MA: Harvard University Press, 2016), 68.

44. Mahmood Mandani, *When Victims Become Killers: Colonialism, Nativism, and the Genocide in Rwanda* (Princeton, NJ: Princeton University Press, 2001), 27.

45. Isin, *Being Political*, 29.

46. Josep Fradera, *The Imperial Nation: Citizens and Subjects in the British, French, Spanish and American Empires* (Princeton, NJ: Princeton University Press, 2018), 111, 152.

47. Lauren Benton, *A Search for Sovereignty: Law and Geography in European Empires 1400–1900* (Cambridge: Cambridge University Press, 2009), 163.

48. Isin, *Being Political*, 204.

49. Christopher Bayly, *Recovering Liberties: Indian Thought in the Age of Liberalism and Empire* (Cambridge: Cambridge University Press, 2011).

50. Elizabeth Kolsky, *Colonial Justice in British India: White Violence and the Rule of Law* (Cambridge: Cambridge University Press, 2010).

51. Balibar, *We, the People of Europe?: Reflections on Transnational Citizenship*, 69.

52. Cooper, *Citizenship between Empire and Nation*, 3.

53. Mimi Sheller, *Democracy after Slavery: Black Publics and Peasant Radicalism in Haiti and Jamaica* (London: Macmillan Education, 2000), 12.

54. Walter Mignolo, *The Darker Side of the Renaissance: Literacy, Territoriality, & Colonization* (Ann Arbor: University of Michigan Press, 2003), 20.

55. Gilroy, *After Empire*, 38.

56. Sheller, *Democracy after Slavery*, 27.

57. Zoë Laidlaw, 'Breaking Britannia's Bounds?: Law, Settlers, and Space in Britain's Imperial Historiography', *The Historical Journal*, Vol. 55, No. 3 (2012): 810.

58. Muller, *Subjects and Sovereign*, 12.

59. See, for example, Alexander Motyl, *Imperial Ends: The Decay, Collapse and Revival of Empire* (New York: Columbia University Press, 2001), 40.

60. Benton, *A Search for Sovereignty*, 161.

61. The implication of Fox's analysis for the historicizing of the spatial aspects of colonialism have been acknowledged by many authors; see, for example, David Levine, *At the Dawn of Modernity: Biology, Culture and Material Life in Europe after the Year 1000* (Los Angeles: University of California Press, 2001), 131, and James Sheehan, 'The Problem of Sovereignty in European History', *American Historical Review*, Vol. 111, No. 1 (2006): 2.

62. Engin Isin, *Citizens without Frontiers* (London: Bloomsbury, 2012), 86.

63. Alan Lester, 'Imperial Circuits and Networks: Geographies of the British Empire', *History Compass*, Vol. 4, No. 1 (2006): 124; Benton, *A Search for Sovereignty*, 17.

CHAPTER 2

1. Ian Haywood, *The Revolution in Popular Literature: Print, Politics and the People, 1790–1860* (Cambridge: Cambridge University Press, 2004), 116.

2. Thomas Metcalfe, *Ideologies of the Raj* (Cambridge: Cambridge University Press, 1994), 28.

3. Partha Chatterjee, *The Black Hole of Empire: History of a Global Practice of Power* (Princeton, NJ: Princeton University Press, 2012), 183, 222.

4. Uday Singh Mehta, *Liberalism and Empire: A Study in Nineteenth Century British Liberal Thought* (Chicago: University of Chicago Press, 1999); Jenifer Pitts, *A Turn to Empire* (Princeton, NJ: Princeton University Press, 2006).

5. The contradictions of liberalism's apparent universalism that Mehta sees arises from the genealogy he uses which begins with Locke and moves to Bentham and the Mills and does not acknowledge the shift from civic republicanism to liberalism in late eighteenth century thought. On the British legal context for this problem, see David Lieberman, *The Province of Legislation Determined: Legal Theory in Eighteenth-Century Britain* (Cambridge: Cambridge University Press, 1990), 18–22.

6. Christopher Bayly, *Recovering Liberties* (Cambridge: Cambridge University Press, 2012); Lynn Zastoupil, *Rammohun Roy and the Making of Victorian Britain* (New York: Palgrave Macmillan, 2011).

7. Thomas Love Peacock, 'Evidence to the Select Committee', delivered on 2 March 1834 in H/536, f. 407, Asian and African Collections, British Library (hereafter AAC).

8. Leicester Stanhope, *Sketch of the History and Influence of the Press in British India* (London: C. Chapple, 1823), 57.

9. Lauren Benton, *Law and Colonial Cultures: Legal Regimes in World History, 1400–1900* (Cambridge: Cambridge University Press, 2002), 129.

10. Nasser Hussien, *Jurisprudence of Emergency* (Cambridge: Cambridge University Press, 2003), 78; this nuances the broad pattern which is discernible through a focus on canonical metropolitan texts. This a starker interpretation of the stratification of the 'citizen' under imperial rule see Anthony Pagden, 'Fellow Citizens and Imperial Subjects: Conquest and Sovereignty in Europe's Overseas Empires', *History and Theory*, Vol. 44, No. 4 (December 2005): 28–46.

11. David Lieberman, *The Province of Legislation Determined: Legal Theory in Eighteenth-Century Britain* (Cambridge: Cambridge University Press, 2010), 1–2.

12. Jon Wilson, *Domination of Strangers: Modern Governance in Eastern India, 1780–1830* (London: Palgrave Macmillan, 2008), 15; Martin J. Wiener expressed skepticism about the endeavor in Bayly's *Recovering Liberalism* to find the 'Indian-ness' of Indian Liberalism. As Wilson and others have shown, such research also uncovers the 'Indian-ness' of 'British Liberalism'. See Martin J. Wiener's contribution to 'Roundtable: Recovering Liberties', *Britain and the World*, Vol. 5, No. 2 (2012): 294–313.

13. Robert Travers, *Ideology and Empire in Eighteenth Century India: The British in Bengal* (Cambridge: Cambridge University Press, 2007).

14. Douglas M. Peers, *Between Mars and Mammon: The Garrison State in British India, 1800 to 1835* (London: I. B. Tauris, 1995); C. A. Bayly, 'The British Military-Fiscal State and Indigenous Resistance, India 1750–1820', in

An Imperial State at War: Britain from 1689 to 1815, ed. Lawrence Stone (New York: Routledge, 1994), 322–54.

15. Lynn Zastoupil, *John Stuart Mill and India* (Stanford, CA: Stanford University Press, 1994), 87–89; Jack Harrington, *Sir John Malcolm and the Creation of British India* (New York: Palgrave Macmillan, 2010), 2–8; Martha Maclaren, *British India & British Scotland, 1780–1830: Career Building, Empire Building, and a Scottish School of Thought on Indian Governance* (Akron, OH: University of Akron Press, 2001).

16. Peers, *Mars and Mammon*, 211; Hussein, *Jurisprudence of Emergency*, 88.

17. Chatterjee, *Black Hole of Empire*, 185–87.

18. Arvind Rajgopal, *The Indian Public Sphere: Readings in Media History* (Oxford: Oxford University Press, 2009), 18.

19. Ibid., p. 10.

20. Jürgen Habermas, *The Structural Transformation of the Public Sphere: Inquiry into a Category of Bourgeois Society* (Gateshead: Athenaeum Press, 1992), 184.

21. Stanhope, *Sketch*, 148.

22. Extract from 'Lieut.-Col. Robison to Chief Secretary, Bengal, 9th June 1822', in H/536, AAC, 565.

23. Zastoupil, *Rammohun Roy*, 101; Kevin Gilmartin, *Print Politics: The Press and Radical Opposition in Early Nineteenth-Century England* (Cambridge: Cambridge University Press, 1996).

24. John Wilkes, *The North Briton from No. 1 to No. XLVI Inclusive* (London: W. Bingley, 1769), 1.

25. James Mill, *Supplement to the Encyclopedia Britannica: Liberty of the Press* (London: J. Innes, 1825), 9.

26. Quoted in Peacock, 'Evidence to the Select Committee', 397.

27. Bayly, *Recovering Liberties*, 100.

28. 'Regulations for the Press, 1799', in H/537, 319.

29. Denis McQuail, *Media Accountability and Freedom of Publication* (Oxford: Oxford University Press, 2003), 34.

30. Penelope Carson, *The East India Company and Religion, 1698–1858* (London: Boydell & Brewer, 2012), 137–39.

31. Sir John Malcolm, *Political History of India, from 1784 to 1823*, Vol. 2 (London: John Murray, 1826), 302.

32. Christopher Bayly, *Empire and Information: Intelligence Gathering and Social Communication in India, 1780–1870* (Cambridge: Cambridge University Press, 1996), 56.

33. 'Plan for a Government Printing Press', 1800 in H/537, AAC, 361.

34. Ibid.

35. Ibid.

36. 'New Rules for the Calcutta Press 16th Oct. 1813', in H/537, AAC, 403.

37. A. F. Salahuddin Ahmed, *Social Ideas and Social Change in Bengal 1818–1835* (Leiden: Brill, 1965), 75–78.
38. The power to banish was confirmed under section 36 of the East India Act 1813.
39. Malcolm, *Political History of India*, Vol. 2, 300.
40. James Silk Buckingham, *The Claims of Mr. Buckingham* (London: His Majesty's Stationery Office, 1826), 8.
41. 'Minute of Governor Elliot on the State of the Indian Press June 1820', H/534, AAC, 347.
42. Cyril Philips, *The East India Company* (Manchester: Manchester University Press, 1960), 182.
43. Buckingham, *Claims*, 64.
44. Thomas Love Peacock, 'Minutes to the Select Committee', 2 June 1834, H/536, AAC, 564.
45. J. H. Harrington, 'Minute by the Honourbale Mr. Harrington, 3 April 1823', in H/533, AAC, 283. During the 1810s and 1820s, Harrington was a leading figure in the development of the legal system in Bengal.
46. See, for example, 'Anti-Native Articles' written under the pseudonym 'Nestor' published by the *Telegraph*, 1799, H537, AAC, 317.
47. Ibid., 318.
48. Spankie to Bailey, 10 March 1823 in H/533, AAC, 219.
49. Quoted in Buckingham, *Claims*, 42.
50. Herbert Compton to Chief Secretary Hill, 20 November 1826 in H/534, 355.
51. Hussein, *Jurisprudence of Emergency*, 78.
52. 'Asiatic Intelligence-Calcutta', in *The Asiatic Journal and Monthly Register for British and Foreign*, Vol. 17 (1835): 87.
53. G. O. Trevelyan, *Life of Lord Macaulay*, Vol. 1 (London: Longman, 1878), 189.
54. Ibid.
55. 'Memorandum from the Governor General in Council to the Court of Directors, dated 17 October 1822', in H353, AAC, 549.
56. Ibid., 55.
57. Elizabeth Kolsky, *Colonial Justice in British India: White Violence and the Rule of Law* (Cambridge: Cambridge University Press, 2010), 22.
58. Robert Travers, 'Contested Despotism: Problems of Liberty in British India', in *Exclusionary Empire*, ed. Jack P. Greene (Cambridge: Cambridge University Press, 2010), 202.
59. On the importance of delegated authority for imperial government, see Lauren Benton, *A Search for Sovereignty: Law and Geography in European Empires 1400–1900* (Cambridge: Cambridge University Press, 2009), 184–87.
60. Thomas Love Peacock, 'Evidence to the Select Committee', 2 June 1834, H/536, AAC, 398.

61. James Silk Buckingham, *The Oriental Herald and Colonial Review*, Vol. 1, 1824, 199.
62. Ibid.
63. Malcolm, *Political History of India*, Vol. 2, 309.
64. Ibid., 312.
65. Stanhope, *Sketch*, 5.
66. Malcolm, *Political History of India*, 318.
67. Wilson, *Domination of Strangers*, 164.
68. 'Asiatic Intelligence', 87.
69. Zastoupil, *Rammohun Roy*, 58.
70. Sir John Malcolm, *Government of India* (London: John Murray, 1833), 187.
71. Malcolm, *Political History of India*, ccxxxviii.
72. Harrington, *Sir John Malcolm and the Creation of British India*, 194.
73. There are many interpretations that emphasis the denial of the capacity of non-Europeans to be subjects of liberal rights *entoto*, see, for example, Mehta, *Liberalism and Empire*.
74. Kolsky, *Colonial Justice*, 32.

CHAPTER 3

1. Derek Heater, *What Is Citizenship?* (Cambridge: Polity Press, 1999).
2. Heater, *What Is Citizenship?*, 4, 44, 115.
3. Hartley Dean, 'A Post-Marshallian Concept of Global Social Citizenship', in *Routledge Handbook of Global Citizenship Studies*, eds. Engin Isin and Peter Nyers (London: Routledge, 2014), 130.
4. Jose Harris, 'Nationality, Rights and Virtue: Some Approaches to Citizenship in Great Britain', in *Lineages of European Citizenship: Rights, Belonging and Participation in Eleven Nation-States*, eds. R. Bellamy, Dario Castiglione, and Emilio Santoro (London: Palgrave Macmillan, 2004), 74.
5. T. H. Marshall, *Citizenship and Social Class: And Other Essays* (Cambridge: Cambridge University Press, 1950).
6. Ibid., 20.
7. Ibid., 22.
8. Ann Dummett and Andrew G. L. Nicol, *Subjects, Citizens, Aliens and Others: Nationality and Immigration Law* (London: Weidenfeld and Nicolson, 1990), 90.
9. Hannah Weiss Muller, *Subjects and Sovereign: Bonds of Belonging in the Eighteenth Century British Empire* (Oxford: Oxford University Press, 2017), 149; Josep Fradera, *The Imperial Nation: Citizens and Subjects in the British, French, Spanish and American Empires* (Princeton, NJ: Princeton University Press, 2018), 99.

10. Mithi Mukherjee, *India in the Shadows of Empire: A Legal and Political History (1774–1950)* (Oxford: Oxford University Press, 2009), ch. 2, 12 [printed from Oxford Scholarship Online, accessed 18 August 2015].

11. Ibid.

12. Adam McKeown, *Melancholy Order: Asian Migration and the Globalization of Borders* (New York: Columbia University Press, 2012), 210.

13. Dummett and Nicol, *Subjects, Citizens, Aliens and Others*, 72.

14. McKeown, *Melancholy Order*, 212.

15. Arnulf Becker Lorca, *Mestizo International Law: A Global Intellectual History, 1842–1933* (Cambridge: Cambridge University Press, 2014), 80–82, 87–89.

16. For some examples of recent critiques of the persistence of Marshall's model, see Guy Ben-Porat and Bryan S. Turner, *The Contradictions of Israeli Citizenship: Land, Religion and State* (London: Routledge, 2011), 3; Kathryn L. Wegner, 'Can There Be a Global Historiography of Citizenship?' in *Routledge Handbook of Global Citizenship Studies*, eds. Engin Isin and Peter Nyers (London: Routledge, 2014), 140.

17. Adrian Favell, *Philosophies of Integration: Immigration and the Idea of Citizenship in France and Britain*, 2nd ed. (London: Palgrave, 2016), 46.

18. Gerard Noiriel, *The French Melting Pot: Immigration, Citizenship and French Identity*, trans. Geoffroy De Lafocarde (Minneapolis: University of Minnesota Press, 1996), 4–7.

19. Noiriel, *The French Melting Pot*, 278.

20. Benjamin Stora, *Les Guerres sans fin: un historien, la France et l'Algérie* (Paris: Pluriel, 2005), 89.

21. Cécile Laborde, 'Republican Citizenship and the Crisis of Integration in France', in *Lineages of European Citizenship: Rights, Belonging and Participation in Eleven Nation-States*, eds. R. Bellamy, Dario Castiglione, and Emilio Santoro (London: Palgrave Macmillan, 2004), 55.

22. Noiriel, *The French Melting Pot*, 91.

23. Maxim Silverman, *Deconstructing the Nation: Immigration, Racism and Citizenship in Modern France* (London: Routledge, 2014), 18; James R. Lehning, *Peasant and French: Cultural Contact in Rural France during the Nineteenth Century* (Cambridge: Cambridge University Press, 1995), 204.

24. Frederick Cooper, *Citizenship, Inequality, and Difference* (Princeton, NJ: Princeton University Press, 2018), 75.

25. Étienne Balibar, *We, The People of Europe?: Reflections on Transnational Citizenship* (Princeton, NJ: Princeton University Press, 2004), 68.

26. This interpretation owes a great deal to Georgios Varouxakis, *Victorian Political Thought on France and the French* (New York: Palgrave Macmillan, 2002), ch. 1.

27. Fradera, *The Imperial Nation*, 50.

28. Fradera, *The Imperial Nation*, 53.

29. John Stuart Mill, 'Duveyrier's Political Views of French Affairs 1846', in *The Collected Works of John Stuart Mill, Volume XX—Essays on French History and Historians*, ed. John M. Robson, intro. John C. Cairns (Toronto: University of Toronto Press; London: Routledge and Kegan Paul, 1985). [Accessed from http://oll.libertyfund.org/title/235/21607 on 15 October 2013].

30. Ibid.

31. Quoted in Varouxakis, *Victorian Political Thought*, 128.

32. Peter Mandler, *Liberty and Authority in Victorian Britain* (Oxford: Oxford University Press, 2006), 79.

33. Robert Tombs and Isabelle Tombs, *That Sweet Enemy: The British and the French from the Sun King to the Present* (London: Pimlico, 2007), 341.

34. David Todd, 'A French Imperial Meridian, 1814–1870', *Past & Present*, Vol. 210, No. 1 (February 2011): 173–75.

35. Abigail Green, 'The British Empire and the Jews: An Imperialism of Human Rights?', *Past & Present*, Vol. 199, No. 2 (2008): 177–79.

36. Lawrence C. Jennings, *French Anti-Slavery: The Movement for the Abolition of Slavery in France* (New York: Cambridge University Press, 2000), 160.

37. Noiriel, *The French Melting Pot*, 210.

38. Priyamvada Gopal, *Insurgent Empire: Anticolonial Resistance and British Dissent* (London: Verso, 2019), 9.

39. Olivier Le Coeur Grandmaison, *Exterminer: Coloniser Sur la guerre et l'Etat colonial* (Paris: Fayard, 2005), 105.

40. Henry Reeve, 'The Sahara and Its Tribes', *Edinburgh Review*, Vol. LXXXIV, July (1846): 75.

41. Karuna Mantena, *Alibis of Empire: Henry Maine and the Ends of Liberal Imperialism* (Princeton, NJ: Princeton University Press, 2010), 141.

42. Jack Harrington, 'Orientalism, Political Subjectivity and the Birth of Citizenship between 1780 and 1830', *Citizenship Studies*, Vol. 16 (2012): 573–86.

43. Saliha Belmessous, *Assimilation and Empire: Uniformity in French and British Colonies, 1541–1954* (Oxford: Oxford University Press, 2014), 3.

44. Osama W. Abi-Mershed, *Apostles of Modernity: Saint-Simonians and the Civilizing Mission in Algeria* (Stanford, CA: Stanford University Press, 2010).

45. Alexis de Tocqueville, *Writings on Empire and Slavery*, ed. Jennifer Pitts (Baltimore, MD: Johns Hopkins University Press, 2000), 207.

46. Laurent Dubois, 'La Republique Metissee: Citizenship, Colonialism, and the Borders of French History', in *Cultural Studies*, Vol. 14, No. 1 (2000): 33.

47. Alejandro E. Gómez, *Le spectre de la révolution noire* (Rennes: Presses universitaires de Rennes, 2013), 7.

48. John Ruedy, *Modern Algeria* (Bloomington: Indiana University Press, 2005), 71.

49. George L. Ditson, *The Crescent and the French Crusaders* (New York: Derby & Jackson, 1859), 275.

50. Varouxakis, *Victorian Political Thought on France and the French*, 166.

CHAPTER 4

1. Anthony Anghie, *Imperialism, Sovereignty and the Making of International Law* (Cambridge: Cambridge University Press, 2004), 53–57; Jessica Marglin, 'Extraterritoriality Meets Islamic Law: Commercial Litigation and Elements of Proof in the International Mixed Court of Morocco, 1871–1872', *Quaderni Storici*, LI, no. 3 (2016): 673–75; Mary Dewhurst Lewis, *Divided Rule: Sovereignty and Empire in French Tunisia, 1881–1938* (Berkeley: University of California Press, 2016).

2. On challenges to this approach, see Cécile Vidal, *Français? La nation en débat entre colonies et métropole, XVIe–XIXe siècle* (Paris: Éditions de l'EHESS, 2014); Gary Wilder, *The French Imperial Nation-State: Negritude and Colonial Humanism between the Two World Wars* (Chicago: University of Chicago Press, 2005).

3. J. Ajzenstat and P. J. Smith (eds.), *Canada's Origins: Liberal, Tory, or Republican?* (Ottawa: Carleton University Press, 1995).

4. J. P. Parry, 'Liberalism and Liberty', in Peter Mandler, *Liberty and Authority in Victorian Britain* (Oxford: Oxford University Press, 2006), 77–80.

5. This revision of Linda Colley's central argument in *Britons: Forging the Nation, 1707–1837* (New Haven, CT: Yale University Press, 1992) is well articulated in works such as Georgios Varouxakis, *Victorian Political Thought on France and the French* (New York: Palgrave Macmillan, 2002); Michael Rapport, *Nationality and Citizenship in Revolutionary France: The Treatment of Foreigners 1789–1799* (Oxford: Oxford University Press, 2000); Peter Sahlins, *Unnaturally French: Foreign Citizens in the Old Regime and After* (Ithaca, NY: Cornell University Press, 2004); Isabelle Tombs and Robert Tombs, *That Sweet Enemy: The British and the French from the Sun King to the Present* (London: Pimlico, 2007).

6. A growing number of works on liberalism and empire have attempted to move beyond the borders of national imperial projects; see, for example, Christopher Bayly, *Recovering Liberties* (Cambridge: Cambridge University Press, 2012); Lauren Benton, *A Search for Sovereignty* (Cambridge: Cambridge University Press, 2009).

7. Zoë Laidlaw, 'Breaking Britannia's Bounds? Law, Settlers, and Space in Britain's Imperial Historiography', *The Historical Journal*, Vol. 55, No. 3 (2012): 819.

8. Elizabeth Thompson, *Colonial Citizens: Republican Rights, Paternal Privilege and Gender in French Syria and Lebanon* (New York: Columbia University Press, 2000); Mary Dewhurst Lewis, 'Geographies of Power: The Tunisian Civic Order, Jurisdictional Politics, and Imperial Rivalry in the Mediterranean, 1881–1935', *Journal of Modern History*, Vol. 80, No. 4 (December 2008).

9. This is surprisingly neglected in the otherwise excellent Varouxakis, *Victorian Political Thought*; recent works on the under-researched protestant dimensions of colonial intellectual history include Robert A. Yelle, *The Language of Disenchantment* (Oxford: Oxford University Press, 2012).

10. John Darwin, *The Empire Project: The Rise and Fall of the British World System, 1830 to 1970* (Cambridge: Cambridge University Press, 2009), 136, 650.

11. Varouxakis, *Victorian Political Thought on France and the French*, 66; Robert Tombs and Isabelle Tombs, *That Sweet Enemy*, 337.

12. Erik Bleich, 'The Legacies of History? Colonization and Immigrant Integration in Britain and France', *Theory and Society*, Vol. 34, No. 2 (April 2005): 171–95.

13. James Lehning, *To Be a Citizen: The Political Culture of the Early French Third Republic* (Ithaca, NY: Cornell University Press, 2001), 128; Rogers Brubaker, *Citizenship and Nationhood in France and Germany* (Cambridge, MA: Harvard University Press, 1992), 86.

14. Karuna Mantena, *Alibis of Empire: Henry Maine and the Ends of Liberal Imperialism* (Princeton, NJ: Princeton University Press, 2010), 148–50; Douglas M. Peers, *Between Mars and Mammon: The Garrison State in British India, 1800 to 1835* (London: I. B. Tauris, 1995), 38; E. D. Steele, *Palmerston and Liberalism, 1855 to 1865* (Cambridge: Cambridge University Press, 1991), 337.

15. Osman Benchérif, *The Image of Algeria in Anglo-American Writing, 1785–1962* (Lanham, MD: University of America Press, 1997), 2–4.

16. Peter Dunwoodie, *Writing French Algeria* (Oxford: Oxford University Press, 1999), especially chapters 2 and 3.

17. See, for example, Uday Singh Mehta, *Liberalism and Empire: A Study in Nineteenth Century British Liberal Thought* (Chicago: University of Chicago Press, 1999); Jennifer Pitts, *A Turn to Empire* (Princeton, NJ: Princeton University Press, 2006).

18. For a thought-provoking example of this approach, see Elaine Hadley, *Living Liberalism: Practicing Citizenship in Mid-Victorian Britain* (Chicago: University of Chicago Press, 2011).

19. Jane Rendall, 'The Condition of Women, Women's Writing and the Empire in Nineteenth-Century Britain', in *At Home with the Empire*, eds. Catherine Hall and Sonya O. Rose (Cambridge: Cambridge University Press, 2006), 105; William Gallois, 'Genocide in Nineteenth-Century Algeria', *Journal of Genocide Research*, Vol. 15, No. 1 (2013): 70; Douglas M. Peers, 'Colonial Knowledge and the Military in India, 1780–1860', *Journal of Imperial and Commonwealth History* 33 (2005): 157–80.

20. Ellen Rogers, *A Winter in Algeria* (London: Sampson Low, Son, and Marston, 1865), 95.

21. Clare Midgely, 'Bridging the Empire Home: Women Activists in Imperial Britain, 1790s–1930s', in *At Home with the Empire*, eds. Catherine Hall and Sonya O. Rose (Cambridge: Cambridge University Press, 2006), 243.

22. See, for example, Joseph Williams Blakesley, *Four Months in Algeria: With a Visit to Carthage* (Cambridge: Macmillan & Co., 1858); Hugh Mulleneux Walmsley, *Sketches of Algeria during the Kabyle war* (London: Chapman and Hall, 1858); James Scott, *A Journal of a Residence in the Esmailla of Abd-el-Kader* (London: Whittaker and Co., 1842). For Scott's role in Abd al-Qādir's army, see Amira K. Bennison, *Jihad and Its Interpretations in Pre-Colonial Morocco* (London: Routledge, 2002), 100–104; John Ruedy, *Modern Algeria* (Bloomington: Indiana University Press, 2005), 58.

23. Andrew Fitzmaurice, 'Anticolonialism in Western Political Thought: The Colonial Origins of the Concept of Genocide', in *Empire, Colony, Genocide: Conquest, Occupation, and Subaltern Resistance in World History*, ed. Dirk Moses (New York: Berghahn Books, 2008), 71.

24. See, for example, George L. Ditson, *The Crescent and the French Crusaders* (New York: Derby & Jackson, 1859), 26; Mabel Crawford, *Through Algeria* (London: Richard Bentley, 1863), i–xv.

25. Pitts, *A Turn To Empire*, 167.

26. George Murray to Robert W. St John, PRO FO112/5, 84. Goderich was the incoming Colonial Secretary following the election of 1830.

27. J. W. Croker, 'Foreign and Domestic Policy', *Quarterly Review*, LXXXIV (1846): 75.

28. Ibid.

29. George Murray to Robert W. St John, PRO FO112/5, 80.

30. J. Spring Rice to Robert W. St John, 25 October 1834, PRO FO112/5, 376.

31. Robert W. St John to Earl Granville, 23 November 1833, PRO FO112/4.

32. Jennifer E. Sessions, *By Sword and Plow: France and the Conquest of Algeria* (Ithaca, NY: Cornell University Press, 2011), chap. 6.

33. Sarah Irving, *Natural Science and the Origins of the British Empire* (London: Chatto & Windus, 2015), 8; Jennifer Pitts, *The Boundaries of the International: Law and Empire* (Cambridge, MA: Harvard University Press, 2018), 139.

34. The translation is my own; Saxe Bannister, *Appel en faveur d'Algerie* (Paris: Dodney-Dupré, 1833), 5.

35. Fitzmaurice, 'Anti-Colonialism', 70.

36. Blakesley, *Four Months*, 44.

37. My translation, Joseph Blakesley, *Four Months*, 38.

38. Ibid., 38.

39. Engels, *Northern Star*.

40. On this debate in the context of Algeria, see Olivier Le Coeur Grandmaison, *Exterminer. Coloniser Sur la guerre et l'Etat colonial* (Paris: Fayard, 2005).

41. Zastoupil, *J. S. Mill's Encounter with India*, 87; Jack Harrington, *Sir John Malcolm and the Creation of British India* (New York: Palgrave Macmillan, 2010), chap. 5.
42. Ditson, *French Crusaders*, 180.
43. Ruedy, *Algeria*, 74.
44. Rogers, *Winter in Algeria*, 49.
45. Blakesley, *Four Months*, 87.
46. Henry Reeve, 'Tribes of the Sahara', *The Edinburgh Review*, Vol. 85 (1846): 71.
47. Ibid.
48. Harrington, *Sir John Malcolm and the Creation of British India*, 57.
49. J. P. Greene (ed.), *Exclusionary Empire: English Liberties Overseas, 1600–1900* (Cambridge: Cambridge University Press, 2009), 7.
50. Georgios Varouxakis, 'Vicotiran Political Thought', 190.
51. Blakesley, *Four Months*, 98.
52. Walmsley, *Sketches*, 100.
53. Ibid.
54. Ruedy, *Algeria*, 74.
55. Sir Grenville Temple, 'Konstantinah in 1837', *The United Service Magazine*, Vol. 30 (1839): 71.
56. Ibid.
57. Ditson, *French Crusaders*, 272.
58. Ibid., 275; see also Mabel Crawford, *Through Algeria*, 358. The parallel with British debates about settler migration is striking.
59. Henry Reeve, 'Tribes of the Sahara', *The Edinburgh Review*, Vol. 85 (1846): 79.
60. J. Harrington, 'Edward Gibbon Wakefield, the Liberal Political Subject and the Settler State', *Journal of Political Ideologies*, Vol. 20, No. 3 (2015): 348.
61. Alan Lester, 'Race and Citizenship', in *The Victorian World*, ed. Martin Hewitt (London: Routledge, 2012), 382.
62. Rogers, *A Winter in Algeria*, 71.
63. Walmsley, *Sketches*, 120.
64. Abigail Green, 'The British Empire and the Jews: An Imperialism of Human Rights?', *Past & Present*, Vol. 199, No. 2 (2008): 126.
65. Albert Memmi, *The Colonizer and the Colonized* (London: Earthscan, 1990), 137.
66. Green, 'The British Empire and the Jews', 130.
67. Grandmaison, 39.
68. Ditson, *French Crusaders*, 17.
69. Ibid., 48.
70. Walmsley, *Sketches*, 199.
71. Harrington, *Sir John Malcolm and the Creation of British India*, 82; Bayly, *Recovering Liberties*, 32.

72. Catherine Hall, 'Writing History, Writing a Nation: Harriet Martineau's *History of the* Peace', in *Harriet Martineau: Authorship, Society and Empire*, eds. Ella Dzelzainis and Cora Kaplan (Manchester: Manchester University Press, 2010), 237.

73. Benchérif, *The Image of Algeria*, 70.

74. Charles Churchill, *The Life of Abdel Kader* (London: Chapman and Hall, 1867), vii.

75. Ibid., 139.

76. Rogers, *A Winter in Algeria*, 70.

77. Ibid., 20.

78. Ditson, *French Crusaders*, 328.

79. Pitts, *A Turn to Empire*, 22.

80. Benton, *A Search for Sovereignty*, 284–85.

81. John Stuart Mill, 'A Few Words on Non-Interference'.

82. Rogers Brubaker, *Citizenship and Nationhood in France and Germany* (Cambridge, MA: Harvard University Press, 1992), 1.

83. Mahmood Mandani, *When Victims Become Killers: Colonialism, Nativism, and the Genocide in Rwanda* (Princeton, NJ: Princeton University Press, 2014), 26.

84. Ruedy, *Algeria*, 75.

85. Sahila Belmessous, *Assimilation and Empire* (Oxford: Oxford University Press, 2012), 130. As Belmessous observes, in the years between the sénatus-consulte and the Cremieux Declaration, Jews were also required to renounce their personal code to become French citizens.

86. Edward Said, *Culture and Imperialism* (London: Chatto & Windus, 1993), 68.

CHAPTER 5

1. Gillian Weiss, *Captives and Corsairs: France and Slavery in the Early Modern Mediterranean* (Stanford, CA: Stanford University Press, 2011), 12; Clancy Smith, *Mediterraneans*, 200.

2. G. Murray to R. W. St. John, 10 January 1831, PRO FO112/05, 91.

3. Lauren Benton, *A Search for Sovereignty: Law and Geography in European Empires 1400–1900* (Cambridge: Cambridge University Press, 2009), 279–84.

4. Sir Grenville Temple, 'Konstantinah in 1837', *The United Service Magazine*, Vol. 30 (1839): 67.

5. C. H. Alexandrowicz, *The Law of Nations in Global History*, eds. David Armitage and Jennifer Pitts (Oxford: Oxford University Press, 2017), 218.

6. Majid Khadduri, 'Islam and the Modern Law of Nations', in *International Law and Islamic Law*, ed. Mashood Baderin (London: Routledge, 2017), 367.

7. Hannah Weiss Muller, *Subjects and Sovereign: Bonds of Belonging in the Eighteenth Century British Empire* (Oxford: Oxford University Press, 2017), 57.

8. Clancy-Smith, *Mediterraneans*, 11, 79.

9. For a recent comprehensive account that puts the Anlgophone world into a comparative context, see James Belich, *Replenishing the Earth: The Settler Revolution and the Rise of the Angloworld* (Oxford: Oxford University Press, 2009).

10. Clancy-Smith, *Mediterraneans*, 14; Benjamin Stora. *La gangrène et l'oubli. La mémoire de la guerre d'Algérie* (Paris: La Decouverte, 2005), 300.

11. Clancy-Smith, *Mediterraneans*, 11; see, for example, Julia Phillips Cohen, *Becoming Ottomans: Sephardi Jews and Imperial Citizenship in the Modern Era* (Oxford: Oxford University Press, 2014).

12. Robert Tombs and Isabelle Tombs, *That Sweet Enemy*, 344.

13. Osman Bencherif, *The Image of Algeria in Anglo-American Writing, 1785–1962* (Lanham, MD: University of America Press, 1997), 22–24.

14. R. W. St John to Sir William Houston, Governor of Gibraltar, 20 November 1831, PRO FO112/04.

15. Elizabeth Broughton, *Six Years Residence in Algeria* (London: Saunders and Otley, 1840), 154; the central role of this narrative in justifying French intervention is discussed in Gillian Weiss, *Captives and Corsairs*.

16. Humphrey Howlett to R. W. St. John, 31 May 1831, PRO FO112/5, 116.

17. T. Spring Rice to R. W. St. John, 17 June 1834, PRO FO112/5, 405.

18. G. Murray to R. W. St. John, 3 January 1830, PRO FO112/5.

19. Henry Reeve, 'Tribes of the Sahara', *The Edinburgh Review*, Vol. 85 (1846): 49.

20. Temple, 'Konstantinah in 1837', 67.

21. Entry for 8 August 1829, 'Consular Diary for Algiers', held at the National Archives, hereafter, PRO FO112/04, 44.

22. On Malta, see J. Clancy Smith, *Mediterraneans*, 79.

23. R. W. St John to Col. Chapman, Chief Secretary, Gibraltar, 29 July 1831, PRO FO112/ 04.

24. R. W. St John to Col. Chapman Chief Secretary, Gibraltar, 29 December 1827, PRO FO122/04, 1–2.

25. R. W. St John to Commander of HMS *Pelorus*, 3 August 1829, FO112/04, 34.

26. Ibid.

27. R. W. St John to Commander of HMS *Pelorus*, 8 August 1829, PRO FO112/04, 34.

28. R. W. St John to Sir Edward Codrington, 16 July 1828, PRO, PRO FO112/04, 15.

29. Smith, *Mediterraneans*, 110.

30. T. Spring Rice to R. W. St John, 17 January 1836, PRO, PRO FO112/05, 407.

31. Drummond Hay HM Agent to Consul General Tangiers 2 September 1840.

32. Consul of Algiers to Sir Hector Geir, 12 March 1840.

33. Stephen Constantine, 'The Pirate, the Governor and the Secretary of State: Aliens, Police and Surveillance in Early Nineteenth-Century Gibraltar', *English Historical Review* (2008) CXXIII (504): 1192.

34. R. W. St John to Col. Chapman Chief Secretary, Gibraltar, 21 September 1829, PRO FO122/04, 45; G. Murray to R. W. St John, 10 January 1831, FO112/05, 91.

35. For such ambiguities in issued passports, see John Torpey, *The Invention of the Passport: Surveillance, Citizenship and the State* (Cambridge: Cambridge University Press, 2000).

36. R. W. St John to Col. Chapman Chief Secretary, Gibraltar, 21 September 1829, PRO FO122/04, 45.

37. Ibid., 46.

38. Abigail Green, 'The British Empire and the Jews: An Imperialism of Human Rights?', *Past & Present*, No. 199 (May 2008): 185.

39. Abigail Green, ibid.; while the law was famously inconsistent on the question of who is a British subject in the first half of the nineteenth century, the assumption that this would include subjects born in Britain's 'European colonies'; Elizabeth Kolsky, *Colonial Justice in British India: White Violence and the Rule of Law*, 104–5.

40. R. W. St John to Governor of Oran, 13 April 1834, FO112/04, 86.

41. G. Murray to R. W. St John, 23 December 1830, FO112/05, 84.

42. T. Spring Rice to R. W. St John, 6 October 1834, FO112/05, 344.

43. G. Murray to R. W. St John, 23 December 1830, FO112/05, 84.

44. Ibid.

45. Lord Grenville to R. W. St John, 24 August 1835, FO112/05, 429.

46. Ibid.

Select Bibliography

Abi-Mershed, Osama W. *Apostles of Modernity: Saint-Simonians and the Civilizing Mission in Algeria* (Stanford, CA: Stanford University Press, 2010).
Adelman, Jeremy. 'What Is Global History?' *Aeon*, 2 March 2017 [Accessed from https://aeon.co/essays/is-global-history-still-possible-or-has-it-had-its-moment on 10 January 2020].
Adib-Moghaddam, Arshin. *A Metahistory of the Clash of Civilisations: Us and Them beyond Orientalism* (Oxford: Oxford University Press, 2011).
Ajzenstat, J., and P. J. Smith (eds.). *Canada's Origins: Liberal, Tory, or Republican?* (Ottawa: Carleton University Press, 1995).
Alexandrowicz, C. H. *The Law of Nations in Global History*. Edited by David Armitage and Jennifer Pitts (Oxford: Oxford University Press, 2017).
Anghie, Anthony. *Imperialism, Sovereignty and the Making of International Law* (Cambridge: Cambridge University Press, 2004).
Anon. 'Asiatic Intelligence-Calcutta'. *The Asiatic Journal and Monthly Register for British and Foreign*, Vol. 17 (1835): 65–99.
Arendt, Hannah. *Origins of Totalitarianism* (New York: Houghton Mifflin Harcourt, 1985).
Balibar, Étienne. *We, the People of Europe? Reflections on Transnational Citizenship* (Princeton, NJ: Princeton University Press, 2004).
Bayly, Christopher. *Empire and Information: Intelligence Gathering and Social Communication in India, 1780–1870* (Cambridge, MA: Cambridge University Press, 1996).
Bayly, Christopher. *The Birth of the Modern World: Global Connections and Comparisons* (London: John Wiley & Sons, 2004).
Bayly, Christopher. *Recovering Liberties: Indian Thought in the Age of Liberalism and Empire* (Cambridge: Cambridge University Press, 2011).

Becker Lorca, Arnulf. *Mestizo International Law: A Global Intellectual History, 1842–1933* (Cambridge: Cambridge University Press, 2014).

Belich, James. *Replenishing the Earth: The Settler Revolution and the Rise of the Angloworld* (Oxford: Oxford University Press, 2009).

Belmessous, Saliha. *Assimilation and Empire: Uniformity in French and British Colonies, 1541–1954* (Oxford: Oxford University Press, 2014).

Benchérif, Osman. *The Image of Algeria in Anglo-American Writing, 1785–1962* (Lanham, MD: University Press of America, 1997).

Bennison, Amira K. *Jihad and Its Interpretations in Pre-Colonial Morocco* (London: Routledge, 2002).

Ben-Porat, Guy, and Bryan S. Turner. *The Contradictions of Israeli Citizenship: Land, Religion and State* (London: Routledge, 2011).

Benton, Laura. *A Search for Sovereignty: Law and Geography in European Empires, 1400–1900* (Cambridge: Cambridge University Press, 2009).

Benton, Lauren. *Law and Colonial Cultures: Legal Regimes in World History, 1400–1900* (Cambridge: Cambridge University Press, 2002).

Benton, Lauren, and Lisa Ford. *Rage for Liberty: The British Empire and the Origins of International Law* (Cambridge, MA: Harvard University Press, 2016).

Blakesley, William. *Four Months in Algeria: With a Visit to Carthage* (Cambridge: Macmillan & Co., 1858).

Bleich, Erik. 'The Legacies of History? Colonization and Immigrant Integration in Britain and France'. *Theory and Society*, Vol. 34, No. 2 (April 2005): 171–95.

Boaventura de Sousa, Santos. *Epistemologies of the South: Justice against Epistemicide* (Boulder, CO: Paradigm Publishing, 2014).

Broughton, Elizabeth. *Six Years Residence in Algeria* (London: Saunders and Otley, 1840).

Brubaker, Rogers. *Citizenship and Nationhood in France and Germany* (Cambridge, MA: Harvard University Press, 1992).

Carson, Penelope. *The East India Company and Religion, 1698–1858* (London: Boydell & Brewer, 2012).

Chatterjee, Partha. *The Black Hole of Empire: History of a Global Practice of Power* (Princeton, NJ: Princeton University Press, 2012).

Churchill, Charles. *The Life of Abdel Kader* (London: Chapman and Hall, 1867).

Colley, Linda. *Britons: Forging the Nation, 1707–1837* (New Haven, CT: Yale University Press, 1992).

Cooper, Frederick. *Citizenship, Inequality, and Difference* (Princeton, NJ: Princeton University Press, 2018).

Crawford, Mabel. *Through Algeria* (London: Richard Bentley, 1863).

Croker, J. W. 'Foreign and Domestic Policy'. *Quarterly Review*, Vol. LXXXIV (1846): 75.

Darwin, John. *After Tamerlane: The Global History of Empire* (London: Penguin, 2007).
Darwin, John. *The Empire Project: The Rise and Fall of the British World System, 1830 to 1970* (Cambridge: Cambridge University Press, 2009).
Dean, Hartley. 'A Post-Marshallian Concept of Global Social Citizenship'. In *Routledge Handbook of Global Citizenship Studies*, edited by Engin Isin and Peter Nyers (London: Routledge, 2014).
Derrida, Jacques. *The Monolingualism of the Other, or the Prosthesis of Origin*. Translated by Patrick Mensah (Stanford, CA: Stanford University Press, 1998).
Devji, Faisal. 'Apologetic Modernity'. *Modern Intellectual History*, Vol. 4, No. 1 (2007): 61–76.
Ditson, George L. *The Crescent and the French Crusaders* (New York: Derby & Jackson, 1859).
Drayton, Richard. 'Where Does the World Historian Write From? Objectivity, Moral Conscience and the Past and Present of Imperialism'. *Journal of Contemporary History*, Vol. 46, No. 3 (2011): 671–85.
Dubois, Laurent. 'La Republique Metissee: Citizenship, Colonialism, and the Borders of French History'. *Cultural Studies*, Vol. 14, No. 1 (2000): 15–34.
Dummett, Ann, and Andrew G. L. Nicol. *Subjects, Citizens, Aliens and Others: Nationality and Immigration Law* (London: Weidenfeld and Nicolson, 1990).
Dunwoodie, Peter. *Writing French Algeria* (Oxford: Oxford University Press, 1999).
Evans, J., P. Grimshaw, D. Philips, and S. Swain. *Equal Subjects, Unequal Rights: Indigenous Peoples in British Settler Colonies 1830–1910* (Manchester: Manchester University Press, 2003).
Evans, Richard J. 'The Demented Dalek'. *London Review of Books*, Vol. 41, No. 17 (12 September 2019). [Accessed online from https://www.lrb.co.uk/the-paper/v41/n17/richard-j.-evans/the-demented-dalek on 15 December 2019].
Favell, Adrian. *Philosophies of Integration Immigration and the Idea of Citizenship in France and Britain* (London: Palgrave Macmillan, 1998).
Ferguson, James. *Anti-Politics Machine: Development, Depoliticization, and Bureaucratic Power in Lesotho* (Minneapolis: University of Minnesota Press, 1994).
Fitzmaurice, Andrew. 'Anticolonialism in Western Political Thought: The Colonial Origins of the Concept of Genocide'. In *Empire, Colony, Genocide: Conquest, Occupation, and Subaltern Resistance in World History*, edited by Dirk Moses (New York: Berghahn Books, 2008).
Fradera, Josep. *The Imperial Nation: Citizens and Subjects in the British, French, Spanish and American Empires* (Princeton, NJ: Princeton University Press, 2018).
Freeden, Michael, and Andrew Vincent (eds.). *Comparative Political Thought: Theorizing Practices* (London: Routledge, 2013).

Gallois, William. 'Genocide in Nineteenth-Century Algeria'. *Journal of Genocide Research*, Vol. 15, No. 1 (2013): 69–88.

Gentleman, Amelia. 'The Week That Took Windrush from Low-Profile Investigation to National Scandal'. *The Guardian*, 18 April 2018.

Gilmartin, Kevin. *Print Politics: The Press and Radical Opposition in Early Nineteenth-Century England* (Cambridge: Cambridge University Press, 1996).

Gilroy, Paul. *After Empire: Postcolonial: Melancholia or Convivial Culture?* (London: Routledge, 2004).

Gómez, Alejandro E. *Le spectre de la révolution noire* (Rennes: Presses universitaires de Rennes, 2013).

Gopal, Priyamvada. *Insurgent Empire: Anticolonial Resistance and British Dissent* (London: Verso, 2019).

Green, Abigail. 'The British Empire and the Jews: An Imperialism of Human Rights?' *Past & Present*, Vol. 199, No. 2 (2008): 175–205.

Greene, Jack P. (ed.). *Exclusionary Empire* (Cambridge: Cambridge University Press, 2010).

Habermas, Jürgen. *The Structural Transformation of the Public Sphere: Inquiry into a Category of Bourgeois Society* (Gateshead: Athenaeum Press, 1992).

Hadley, Elaine. *Living Liberalism: Practical Citizenship in Mid-Victorian Britain* (Chicago: University of Chicago Press, 2010).

Hall, Catherine. *Civilising Subjects: Metropole and Colony in the English Imagination, 1830–1867* (London: Polity, 2002).

Hall, Catherine. 'Writing History, Writing a Nation: Harriet Martineau's *History of the Peace*'. In *Harriet Martineau: Authorship, Society and Empire*, edited by Ella Dzelzainis and Cora Kaplan (Manchester: Manchester University Press, 2010).

Hall, Catherine. 'Mother Country'. *London Review of Books*, Vol. 42, No. 2 (2020): 11–14.

Harrington, Jack. 'Orientalism, Political Subjectivity and the Birth of Citizenship between 1780 and 1830'. *Citizenship Studies*, Vol. 16 (2012): 573–86.

Harrington, Jack. *Sir John Malcolm and the Creation of British India* (New York: Palgrave Macmillan, 2010).

Harris, Jose. 'Nationality, Rights and Virtue: Some Approaches to Citizenship in Great Britain'. In *Lineages of European Citizenship: Rights, Belonging and Participation in Eleven Nation-States*, edited by R. Bellamy, Dario Castiglione, and Emilio Santoro (London: Palgrave Macmillan, 2004).

Hartkopf Schloss, Rebecca. *Sweet Liberty: The Final Days of Slavery in Martinque* (Philadelphia: University of Pennsylvania Press, 2009).

Heater, Derek. *What Is Citizenship?* (London: John Wiley & Sons, 1999).

Hussien, Nasser. *Jurisprudence of Emergency* (Cambridge: Cambridge University Press, 2003).

Irving, Sarah. *Natural Science and the Origins of the British Empire* (London: Chatto & Windus, 2015).
Isin, Engin. *Being Political: Genealogies of Citizenship* (London: University of Minnesota Press, 2002).
Isin, Engin. *Citizens without Frontiers* (London: Bloomsbury, 2012).
Isin, Engin. 'Theorizing Acts of Citizenship'. In *Acts of Citizenship*, edited by Engin Isin and Greg Nielsen (Chicago: University of Chicago Press, 2008).
Isin, Engin, and Peter Nyers (eds.). *Routledge Handbook of Citizenship Studies* (London: Routledge, 2014).
Ivison, Duncan. 'Justice and Imperialism: On the Very Idea of a Universal Standard'. In *Law and Politics in British Colonial Thought: Transpositions of Empire*, edited by Shaunnagh Dorsett and Ian Hunter (Basingstoke: Palgrave Macmillan, 2010).
Jayawardena, Kumari. *Feminism and Nationalism in the Third World* (London: Zed Books, 1986).
Jennings, Lawrence C. *French Anti-Slavery: The Movement for the Abolition of Slavery in France* (New York: Cambridge University Press, 2000).
Khadduri, Majid. 'Islam and the Modern Law of Nations'. In *International Law and Islamic Law*, edited by Mashood Baderin (London: Routledge, 2017).
Kolsky, Elizabeth. *Colonial Justice in British India: White Violence and the Rule of Law* (Cambridge: Cambridge University Press, 2010).
Kymlicka, Will. *Multicultural Citizenship: A Liberal Theory of Minority Rights* (Oxford: Oxford University Press, 1995).
Laborde, Cécile. 'Republican Citizenship and the Crisis of Integration in France'. In *Lineages of European Citizenship: Rights, Belonging and Participation in Eleven Nation-States*, edited by R. Bellamy, Dario Castiglione, and Emilio Santoro (London: Palgrave Macmillan, 2004).
Laidlaw, Zoë. 'Breaking Britannia's Bounds? Law, Settlers, and Space in Britain's Imperial Historiography'. *The Historical Journal*, Vol. 55, No. 3 (September 2012): 807–30.
Le Coeur Grandmaison, Olivier. *Exterminer: Coloniser Sur la guerre et l'Etat colonial* (Paris: Fayard, 2005).
Lehning, James R. *Peasant and French: Cultural Contact in Rural France during the Nineteenth Century* (Cambridge: Cambridge University Press, 1995).
Lehning, James R. *To Be a Citizen: The Political Culture of the Early French Third Republic* (Ithaca, NY: Cornell University Press, 2001).
Lester, Alan. 'Race and Citizenship'. In *The Victorian World*, edited by Martin Hewitt (London: Routledge, 2012).
Levine, David. *At the Dawn of Modernity: Biology, Culture and Material Life in Europe after the Year 1000* (Los Angeles: University of California Press, 2001).

Lewis, Mary Dewhurst. *Divided Rule: Sovereignty and Empire in French Tunisia, 1881–1938* (Berkeley: University of California Press, 2016).

Lewis, Mary Dewhurst. 'Geographies of Power: The Tunisian Civic Order, Jurisdictional Politics, and Imperial Rivalry in the Mediterranean, 1881–1935'. *Journal of Modern History*, Vol. 80, No. 4 (December 2008): 791–830.

Lieberman, David. *The Province of Legislation Determined: Legal Theory in Eighteenth Century Britain* (Cambridge: Cambridge University Press, 1990).

MacKenzie, John M. '"Comfort" and "Conviction": A Response to Bernard Porter'. *Journal of Imperial and Commonwealth History*, Vol. 36, No. 4 (2008): 659–68.

Maclaren, Martha. *British India & British Scotland, 1780–1830: Career Building, Empire Building, and a Scottish School of Thought on Indian Governance* (Akron, OH: University of Akron Press, 2001).

Magnette, Paul. *Citizenship: The History of an Idea* (Colchester: ECPR, 2005).

Malcolm, Sir John. *Government of India* (London: John Murray, 1833).

Malcolm, Sir John. *Political History of India, from 1784 to 1823*, 2 Vols. (London: John Murray, 1826).

Manby, Bronwen. *Citizenship and Statelessness in Africa: The Law and Politics of Belonging* (Oisterwijk: Wolf Legal Publishing, 2015).

Mandani, Mahmood. *When Victims Become Killers: Colonialism, Nativism, and the Genocide in Rwanda* (Princeton, NJ: Princeton University Press, 2014).

Mandler, Peter. *Liberty and Authority in Victorian Britain* (Oxford: Oxford University Press, 2006).

Manela, Erez. *The Wilsonian Moment: Self-Determination and the International Origins of Anticolonial Nationalism* (London: Oxford University Press, 2007).

Mantena, Karuna. *Alibis of Empire: Henry Maine and the Ends of Liberal Imperialism* (Princeton, NJ: Princeton University Press, 2010).

Marglin, Jessica. 'Extraterritoriality Meets Islamic Law: Commercial Litigation and Elements of Proof in the International Mixed Court of Morocco, 1871–1872'. *Quaderni Storici*, Vol. LI, No. 3 (2016): 673–700.

Marshall, T. H. *Citizenship and Social Class: And Other Essays* (Cambridge: Cambridge University Press, 1950).

McKeown, Adam. *Melancholy Order: Asian Migration and the Globalization of Borders* (New York: Columbia University Press, 2012).

McQuail, Denis. *Media Accountability and Freedom of Publication* (Oxford: Oxford University Press, 2003).

Mehta, Uday Singh. *Liberalism and Empire: A Study in Nineteenth Century British Liberal Thought* (Chicago: University of Chicago Press, 1999).

Mendieta, Eduardo. 'Freedom as Practice and Civic Genius: On James Tully's Public Philosophy'. In *Freedom and Democracy in an Imperial Context*, edited by Robert Nichols and Jakeet Singh (Abingdon: Routledge, 2014).

Midgley, Clare. 'Bridging the Empire Home: Women Activists in Imperial Britain, 1790s–1930s'. In *At Home with the Empire*, edited by Catherine Hall and Sonya O. Rose (Cambridge: Cambridge University Press, 2006).

Mignolo, Walter. 'The Geopolitics of Knowledge and the Colonial Difference'. *The South Atlantic Quarterly* (Winter 2002): 57–96.

Mill, James. *Supplement to the Encyclopedia Britannica: Liberty of the Press* (London: J. Innes. 1825).

Mill, John Stuart. 'Duveyrier's Political Views of French Affairs 1846'. In *The Collected Works of John Stuart Mill, Volume XX—Essays on French History and Historians*, edited by John M. Robson, introduction by John C. Cairns (Toronto: University of Toronto Press; London: Routledge and Kegan Paul, 1985). [Accessed from http://oll.libertyfund.org/title/235/21607 on 15 October 2013].

Motyl, Alexander. *Imperial Ends: The Decay, Collapse and Revival of Empire* (New York: Columbia University Press, 2001).

Mukherjee, Mithi. *India in the Shadows of Empire: A Legal and Political History (1774–1950)* (Oxford: Oxford University Press, 2009).

Ndiaye, Pap. *La condition noire: Essai sur une minorité française* (Paris: Broché, 2009).

Nichols, Robert, and Jakeet Singh (eds.). *Freedom and Democracy in an Imperial Context* (Abingdon: Routledge, 2014).

Noiriel, Gérard. *The French Melting Pot: Immigration, Citizenship and French Identity*. Translated by Geoffroy De Lafocarde (Minneapolis: University of Minnesota Press, 1996).

Pagden, Anthony. 'Fellow Citizens and Imperial Subjects: Conquest and Sovereignty in Europe's Overseas Empires'. *History and Theory*, Vol. 44, No. 4 (December 2005): 28–46.

Paul, Kathleen. *Whitewashing Britain: Race and Citizenship in the Postwar Era* (Ithaca, NY: Cornell University Press, 1997).

Peers, Douglas M. *Between Mars and Mammon: The Garrison State in British India, 1800 to 1835* (London: I. B. Tauris, 1995).

Peers, Douglas M. 'Colonial Knowledge and the Military in India, 1780–1860'. *Journal of Imperial and Commonwealth History*, Vol. 33 (2005): 157–80.

Philips, Cyril. *The East India Company* (Manchester: Manchester University Press, 1960).

Phillips Cohen, Julia. *Becoming Ottomans* (Oxford: Oxford University Press, 2014).

Pitts, Jennifer. *The Boundaries of the International: Law and Empire* (Cambridge, MA: Harvard University Press, 2018).

Pitts, Jennifer. *A Turn to Empire* (Princeton, NJ: Princeton University Press, 2006).

Porter, Bernard. *The Absent-Minded Imperialists: Empire, Society, and Culture in Britain* (Oxford: Oxford University Press, 2004).

Rajgopal, Arvind. *The Indian Public Sphere: Readings in Media History* (Oxford: Oxford University Press, 2009).

Rao, Rahul. *Third World Protest: Between Home and the World* (Oxford: Oxford University Press, 2010).

Rapport, Michael. *Nationality and Citizenship in Revolutionary France: The Treatment of Foreigners 1789–1799* (Oxford: Oxford University Press, 2000).

Reeve, Henry. 'The Sahara and Its Tribes'. *Edinburgh Review*, Vol. LXXXIV (July 1846): 47–75.

Rendall, Jane. 'The Condition of Women, Women's Writing and the Empire in Nineteenth-Century Britain'. In *At Home with the Empire*, edited by Catherine Hall and Sonya O. Rose (Cambridge: Cambridge University Press, 2006).

Rogers, Ellen. *A Winter in Algeria* (London: Sampson Low, Son, and Marston, 1865).

Ruedy, John. *Modern Algeria* (Bloomington: Indiana University Press, 2005).

Sahlins, Peter. *Unnaturally French: Foreign Citizens in the Old Regime and After* (Ithaca, NY: Cornell University Press, 2004).

Said, Edward. *Culture and Imperialism* (London: Chatto & Windus, 1993).

Salahuddin Ahmed, A. F. *Social Ideas and Social Change in Bengal 1818–1835* (Leiden: Brill, 1965).

Scott, James. *A Journal of a Residence in the Esmailla of Abd-el-Kader* (London: Whittaker and Co., 1842).

Sessions, Jennifer S. *By Sword and Plow: France and the Conquest of Algeria* (Ithaca, NY: Cornell University Press, 2011).

Sheehan, James. 'The Problem of Sovereignty in European History'. *American Historical Review*, Vol. 111, No. 1 (2006): 1–15.

Sheller, Mimi. *Democracy after Slavery: Black Publics and Peasant Radicalism in Haiti and Jamaica* (London: Macmillan Education, 2000).

Silk Buckingham, James. *The Claims of Mr. Buckingham* (London: His Majesty's Stationery Office, 1826).

Silk Buckingham, James. *The Oriental Herald and Colonial Review*, Vol. 1 (1824).

Silverman, Maxim. *Deconstructing the Nation: Immigration, Racism and Citizenship in Modern France* (London: Routledge, 2014).

Skinner, Quentin. 'Two Concepts of Citizenship'. *Tijdschrift voor Filosofie*, 55ste Jaarg., Nr. 3 (1993): 403–419.

Stanhope, Leicester. *Sketch of the History and Influence of the Press in British India* (London: C. Chapple, 1823).

Steele, E. D. *Palmerston and Liberalism, 1855 to 1865* (Cambridge: Cambridge University Press, 1991).

Stone, Lawrence (ed.). *An Imperial State at War: Britain from 1689 to 1815* (New York: Routledge, 1994).

Stora, Benjamin. *La gangrène et l'oubli. La mémoire de la guerre d'Algérie* (Paris: La Découverte, 2005).
Stora, Benjamin. *Les Guerres sans fin: un historien, la France et l'Algérie* (Paris: Pluriel, 2005).
Temple, Sir Grenville. 'Konstantinah in 1837'. *The United Service Magazine*, Vol. 30 (1839): 27–39.
Thompson, Elizabeth. *Colonial Citizens: Republican Rights, Paternal Privilege and Gender in French Syria and Lebanon* (New York: Columbia University Press, 2000).
de Tocqueville, Alexis. *Writings on Empire and Slavery*. Edited by Jennifer Pitts (Baltimore, MD: Johns Hopkins University Press, 2000).
Todd, David. 'A French Imperial Meridian, 1814–1870'. *Past & Present*, Vol. 210, No. 1 (February 2011): 155–86.
Tombs, Robert, and Isabelle Tombs. *That Sweet Enemy: The British and the French from the Sun King to the Present* (London: Pimlico, 2007).
Torpey, John. *The Invention of the Passport: Surveillance, Citizenship and the State* (Cambridge: Cambridge University Press, 2000).
Travers, Robert. *Ideology and Empire in Eighteenth Century India: The British in Bengal* (Cambridge: Cambridge University Press, 2007).
Trevelyan, G. O. *Life of Lord Macaulay* (London: Longman, 1878).
Tully, James. *Public Philosophy in a New Key*, Vol. 1 (Cambridge: Cambridge University Press, 2008).
Turner, Joe. 'Internal Colonisation: The Intimate Circulations of Empire, Race and Liberal Government'. *European Journal of International Relations*, Vol. 24, No. 4 (2018): 765–90.
Varouxakis, Georgios. *Victorian Political Thought on France and the French* (New York: Palgrave Macmillan, 2002).
Vidal, Cécile. *Français? La nation en débat entre colonies et métropole, XVIe-XIXe siècle* (Paris: Éditions de l'EHESS, 2014).
Walmsley, Hugh Mulleneux. *Sketches of Algeria during the Kabyle War* (London: Chapman and Hall, 1858).
Warren, Rosie (ed.). *The Debate on Postcolonial Theory and the Spectre of Capital* (London: Verso, 2017).
Wegner, Kathryn L. 'Can There Be a Global Historiography of Citizenship?' In *Routledge Handbook of Global Citizenship Studies*, edited by Engin Isin and Peter Nyers (London: Routledge, 2014).
Weill, Patrick. *How to Be a French Citizen* (Durham, NC: Duke University Press, 2008).
Weiss, Gillian. *Captives and Corsairs: France and Slavery in the Early Modern Mediterranean* (Stanford, CA: Stanford University Press, 2011).
Weiss Muller, Hannah. *Subjects and Sovereign: Bonds of Belonging in the Eighteenth Century British Empire* (Oxford: Oxford University Press, 2017).

Wiener, Martin J. 'Roundtable: Recovering Liberties'. *Britain and the World*, Vol. 5, No. 2 (2012): 294–313.

Wilder, Gary. *The French Imperial Nation-State: Negritude and Colonial Humanism between the Two World Wars* (Chicago: University of Chicago Press, 2005).

Wilkes John. *The North Briton from No. 1 to No. XLVI Inclusive* (London: W. Bingley, 1769).

Wilson, Jon. *Domination of Strangers: Modern Governance in Eastern India, 1780–1830* (London: Palgrave Macmillan, 2008).

Yelle, Robert A. *The Language of Disenchantment* (Oxford: Oxford University Press, 2012).

Zastoupil, Lynn. *John Stuart Mill and India* (Stanford, CA: University of Stanford Press, 1994).

Zastoupil, Lynn. *Rammohun Roy and the Making of Victorian Britain* (New York: Palgrave Macmillan, 2011).

Index

Algeria: comparisons with India (*see* India); France and, 14; independence of, 15, 19, 59; invasion of, 69–71, 73, 77; Jewish people and, 10; model of colonization, 1, 5, 35, 63–67, 72, 79–82; Young Algerian movement and, 19
Algiers, 6, 10, 19, 73–81, 85, 87–97
American Revolution, 11
Amherst, William Pitt, 41
anticolonial movements, 15, 17, 19, 23, 26–29
Arendt, Hannah, 1–2, 20, 102
Article 4 (2005), 14
Atlantic world, 25, 32, 61, 66
Australia, 5

Balibar, Étienne, 17, 26, 59–60
Bannister, Saxe, 62, 76
Bayly, C. A., 18
Bentinck, William Cavendish, 34
British empire: comparison with French empire, 2, 5, 9, 13–14, 17, 19, 22, 63–65; historiography of, 2, 15

British India. *See* India
British subjects, 23, 31; in Algeria, 86, 89–96; of Malta (*see* Maltese people)

Canada, 5, 27, 55
Césaire, Aimé, 14
citizenship: aspects of, 12; British models of, 53–57, 62–66; Eurocentric ideas of, 13, 16, 17; exclusion and, 21, 25; French models of, 26–27, 58–66, 74, 80; history of, 22; imperial, 3, 17, 19, 51–52, 57, 60–66, 71, 80–86, 97, 100–102; subjecthood and, 6, 10, 23–24, 28, 57, 60–67, 71
Code de l'indigénat, 25
colonial violence, 1, 19, 32, 63, 73, 77, 83, 101
Cooper, Frederick, 17, 18, 48, 59, 62, 70, 81, 89
Crémieux Decree, 10
critical citizenship studies, 12, 18, 20, 24, 27

Derrida, Jacques, 10, 21

East India Company, 26–27, 34–37, 55
European Union, 6, 12

Fanon, Frantz, 25
freedom of the press, 4–5, 31, 32–49
French empire: Christian identity of, 6; comparison with British empire (*see* British empire); Vichy regime and, 10
French republicanism. *See* republicanism
French Revolution, 1
French subjects, 10, 24–28, 39, 84, 100

garrison state. *See* militarism
gender, 17, 54, 66, 100
gens de couleur, 24
Gilroy, Paul, 17, 27
Global South, 17
Gove, Michael, 14

Haiti, 26
Ho Chi Minh, 15

imperial citizenship. *See* citizenship
India, 4, 19, 51, 55–56, 63–67, 99; comparisons with Algeria, 69, 71, 73, 77–81, 100–101; freedom of the press in, 25–27, 31–49
international law, 17, 62, 74, 76, 86–87, 95, 97
Iraq, invasion of, 14
Isin, Engin, 20–21

Jamaica, 26, 55
Jewish Emancipation, 19, 55, 80
Jewish people, 10, 12, 23, 58, 62, 72, 79, 83, 84, 86, 88, 90, 93–96

Kenyatta, Jomo, 15

Lenin, Vladimir Ilyich Ulyanov, 1
Levinas, Emmanuel, 20
liberalism, 2, 5, 26, 31–33, 36–39, 41, 43, 45–49, 61, 67

Macaulay, Thomas Babington, 43, 45
Maine, Sire Henry, 64
Malcolm, Sir John, 34, 41, 44–48, 64
Malta. *See* Maltese people
Maltese people, 19, 55, 72, 86, 88, 90–93, 96
Marshall, T. H., 53–57, 66
Marx, Karl, 87
metropole, 5, 19, 25, 28–29, 33, 42, 44, 48, 52, 61, 63–64, 66–71, 74, 78–79, 84, 86, 93–94, 97–101
militarism, 5, 25–26, 34–36, 39, 41, 47–48, 61, 63, 67, 69, 72–75, 76–81, 83, 89, 97
Mill, James, 37, 47
Mill, John Stuart, 61, 72, 83
Milton, John, 37
Mughals, 27, 33
Munro, Sir Thomas, 34, 41, 44, 64

Napoleon, Louis: Napoleon III, 64, 71, 78; Napoleonic wars, 31, 61, 88
Ndiaye, Pap, 10
Nehru, Jawaharlal, 15
New Zealand, 5
Noiriel, Gérard, 10, 58–59
non-citizens, 12, 20
North Africa, 14

orientalism, 3, 68, 79
Ottoman empire, 6, 24, 57, 80, 87–89, 92, 95

postcolonialism: citizenship and, 11, 15, 22, 24; theories of, 13, 15, 17, 21, 101
postcolonial states, 2, 4, 15, 16

race, 9, 11, 16–17, 20, 24, 26, 32–33, 55, 57, 60, 66, 69, 80, 100
Reeve, Henry, 77, 79, 90
republicanism, 2, 15, 17, 32, 51, 53, 59–61, 65–71, 81
Rogers, Ellen, 72, 77, 81–84, 91
Roy, Ram Mohan, 33, 36, 46–47

Said, Edward, 84
Scott, Sir Walter, 81
settlers, 1, 28, 62, 64–67, 70, 78–79, 100
slavery, 62, 64–67, 89, 94
social citizenship

Spivak, Gayatri, 15–16, 19, 21
Stora, Benjamin, 14, 59
subjects. *See* British subjects; French subjects

de Tocqueville, Alexis, 63, 65, 83, 90
Trinidad and Tobago, 27, 55

Vichy regime, 10

Wellesley, Richard, 38, 39, 47, 48
Wellington, First Duke of, 74
Windrush scandal, 11

About the Author

Jack Harrington manages humanities and social science research at the Wellcome Trust.